I0125257

ISBN-13: 978-0692804148
ISBN-10: 0692804145

DEDICATION

To my parents, siblings, extended family, teachers, mentors,
colleagues, and especially to all the children, parents, and families
who have trusted me to walk with them on their journeys toward
health, happiness, and growth.

CONTENTS

Dedication

Acknowledgments

Introduction

1. Professional Identity 9
   Website
   Practice Information
   Client Forms
   Philosophy
   Mission and Vision

2. Practice Model 12
   Intake
   Practice Model
   Informed Consent
   First Session
   Payment

3. Psychoeducation 17
   Second Session
   Psychoeducation
   Trauma
   Brain Development
   Child Attachment
   Adult Attachment
   Developmental Stages
   Grief and Loss
   Therapeutic Parenting

4. Adult Attachment Interview 24
   Conducting the Interview
   Interpreting the Answers
   Adult Attachment Styles
   Exploring Triggers
   Exploring Expectations

Learning Styles
Adult Attachment Interview

5. Treatment Planning 31
   Goals
   Attachment Trauma Treatment Plan
   Parent Role
   Parent Expectations
   PACE of Therapy
   Preparing the Child
   Diagnosis

6. Family Therapy 37
   Introducing Therapy
   Informed Consent
   Strengths Finding
   Claiming Narrative
   Illustrating Attachment
   Hurt Heart
   Assessment of Relationship
   Self-Disclosure

7. Emotional Intelligence 46
   Hand/Brain Demonstration
   Feelings Book
   Feelings Candyland
   Scaling Emotions
   Puppets

8. Trauma Therapy 55
   Family History
   Trauma Book
   Role Play
   Trauma Narrative
   Trauma Metaphors

9. Coping Skills 63
   Angry Volcano
   Angry Sponges

Theraplay
Power of Silence

10. Self Esteem 68
    Therapeutic Joining
    Success Narrative
    Self Esteem Book
    Core Belief System
    Down in the Hole
    Play Therapy
    School Focus

11. Problem Solving 74
    Identifying Patterns
    Connecting to Trauma
    Identifying Needs
    Lying
    Stealing
    Aggression
    Manipulation
    Family Chart
    Parenting Style
    Emergency Services

12. Evaluation/Termination 87
    Evaluation Questions
    Restate of Confidentiality
    Appreciation of Relationship
    Closing Ritual
    Sticking Points

13. Nuts and Bolts 92
    Office
    Leases
    Telephone
    Voice Mail
    Computer
    Website
    Billing Programs

Accounting Program
Forms
Furniture
E-mail
Facsimile
Scanner
Credit Cards
Books
Games
Toys
Markers
Supplies
Sand Tray
Play House
License
Continuing Education
Business Tax
Business Insurance
Malpractice Insurance
Insurance Panels
Insurance Billing
Accounting Programs
Electronic Billing
Electronic Files
Referrals
Paper Files
Banking
Storage

Epilogue 101

Bibliography 104

Appendices 109
Policies and Procedures
Intake Form
Informed Consent
Notice of Privacy Practices
Authorization for Release/Exchange of Information

Michael A. Jones, LCSW

Assessment
Progress Note
Legal/Ethical
Discharge Summary
Discharge Letter
Family Chart

About the Author

ACKNOWLEDGMENTS

Credit goes to my colleagues who have shared their practice tools and wisdom with me and to the scientists, social workers, clinicians, and professors cited in the bibliography who have contributed to my understanding of family issues and how to address them.

TEN YEARS PRACTICE

Introduction

Private Practice. That was the pinnacle of success I saw when I decided to change careers and become a social worker. Private, because it was something that would belong to me, my own creation I would pursue without interference after years of working for media companies and at the whim of whatever news director was in charge at the time. This kind of independence runs in the family. My family was farmers used to planting their own crops, butchering their own animals, building their own homes. Only after farming failed and World War II ended did my grandfathers go to work for the railroad and an ordinance plant to bring home union paychecks. My father tried all that but chafed under the supervision of corporate bosses and union chiefs. So, he went from pool hall owner to repo man to delivering propane to heating and air conditioning with independent efforts at running a hardware store and real estate scattered in between. He liked making his own decisions and making his own hours. It's not a surprise then that all five of his children are either in business for ourselves or have carved out unique and independent roles in service to others just like our mother, a registered nurse.

Private also means, to some extent, solitary. Certainly, private practice can include working in a group, with other therapists and disciplines, or for a company providing mental health services. But for me private practice meant owning my own business as a sole proprietor or limited liability corporation. Which means that decisions from advertising to office space, client referrals to specialized training, to risk assessment, mandated reporting, treatment planning, and intervention strategies are mine to make. With this privilege comes power, and with this power comes liability, and with this liability comes a certain amount of stress, separate from the stress of managing finances, which is often an inside joke among social workers, but rather serious business when your living depends on the literal ebb and flow of income and expenses. A saying sticks with me from business books to military training to a law and ethics training by Gerry Grossman: "Never worry alone."

Maya Angelou describes standing on the shoulders of those who have gone before and of feeling backed by those who have supported us on our way. I have been lucky to have had many of those mentors starting with my own parents and teachers. In television as in other industries the moto is "fake it 'til you make it." So, when I started reporting the news I would "channel" Barbara Walters asking serious questions of those in authority or my journalism professor at the University of Missouri, Columbia, Dan Dugan, in writing and Walter Cronkite in pacing my delivery. During my master of social work studies at Our Lady of the Lake University in San Antonio, Texas, I had the excellent examples of my field instructors. Ed Cardenas at J.T. Brackenridge Elementary School could calm a group of hyperactive boys just by walking in the room. At Catholic Charities of San Antonio Arlis Schmidt took me for a Coke after a particularly triggering run-in with a nun. At Child Welfare Services in San Diego my LCSW supervisor Becki DeBont would simply say, "And the mirror appears", emphasizing the need for self-reflection. Supervisor Laurie Adam would back me to the hilt when I disagreed with management about adoption recommendations. Also at Child Welfare Services, first Renee Smylie then Karen Martin turned me loose to create an internship program that taught me more than anything I had to offer students. When I did put my foot in the water of private practice after earning my license Nancy North, LCSW was there to hold my hand. Then I landed in an office with exceptional therapists who had already made the leap from Children's Hospital. Chris Diani, LCSW, Laurie Hall, LCSW, and Deborah Holmes, LCSW shared everything from a practice philosophy to the forms and paperwork to get started on my own. To this day there is a safety net of colleagues with whom to consult and complain.

The practice part puts you at the party with doctors, lawyers, and other professionals who have degrees, licenses, offices, billing, and malpractice insurance. "My practice," sounds like you have arrived. It sounds trite to say that practice is not an end but a beginning and just as trite to say that practice makes perfect. There can be no end to learning about the nature of humans, our strengths and challenges and what works to apply one to the other. And there can be no perfection in the joining of unique individuals except in the joy of doing so. Practice, then, is not a noun but a verb that indicates the act of applying knowledge and experience from our education and training with consultation and supervision to the life experiences and personal wisdom of clients with the intention to help as much as necessary while hurting as little as possible. It is also cliché to say that these human services, from customer care to nursing, from sales to psychotherapy, are as much art as science. But despite the efforts of industrial science to quantify human interaction and research into human behavior to develop evidenced-based practice, there is qualitative research to indicate it takes some time to achieve mastery. Popular media quote 10-thousand hours to achieve mastery in one's field, approximately five years at 40-hours a week with two weeks off for vacation. If that is true, I achieved mastery in 2011. But I and most of my colleagues would say we have achieved some level of competence but nowhere near perfection.

Why, you may ask, did you switch from a lucrative career in television reporting to a completely different career in the profitable field of social work? (Tongue planted firmly in cheek.) My answer is that they are essentially the same job. As a reporter I was expected to respond to crisis situations; fires, floods, tornadoes, murders, political disputes both major and mundane. I had to find the source; the victim, the perpetrator, the authority. And, with nothing but a pad and pen, and oh yes, a camera and a microphone, convince them to tell me their story. I had to ask very personal questions of complete strangers in a way that would reveal the truth of their circumstances. Then, under deadline pressure, turn this raw data into an assessment of sorts, a compelling narrative with a beginning, middle, and end in the space of a minute and thirty seconds. Those stories aired on the evening 6:00 p.m. or late night 11 p.m. newscast could entertain, educate, and sometimes challenge people and organizations to change. Not all of them in 15 years were Emmy-winning, in fact none were, but they did get some attention, some a lot. For some reason, after a time, I was either assigned or volunteered to find and interview the victims and family members of the disaster of the day.

In April 1992, it was the family of one of four young people lined up inside a walk-in cooler and shot in the back of the head execution style at a Lee's Famous Recipe Chicken restaurant in Tulsa, Oklahoma. The mother of the 15-year-old boy let me in the front door. The very top of the living room walls was lined with pen and ink and watercolor drawings. It was the work of her son. It was his story I told that night on the news. I sat with her and the other family members as the suspects were put on trial and convicted, then I went on to cover the election of President Bill Clinton, lots of 4th of

July parades, and the bombing of the Alfred P. Murrah Federal Building in Oklahoma City.

In 1998, as I was starting my graduate education in social work I was sitting at the assignment desk one Saturday morning at KSAT-TV, the ABC affiliate in San Antonio, Texas where I was working part time. In the morning mail, there was an envelope addressed to me personally. I opened the envelope and out fell two letters, each written two years apart, and a picture of a woman with long brown hair standing in front of a bright orange Corvette. I had no clue who the woman was or how she found me. This was before Google searches and Facebook. The woman was writing to thank me for my work in showing compassion and telling the story of her son who was one of the victims of the chicken shop shooting. And then I remembered. She had shown me the shell of a vehicle in the garage that day that was to be her son's first car. But he did not live to be 16 and get his driver's license, and so she and her husband completed the project and toured car shows with the restored Corvette in his honor. My lesson: people can survive tragedy and grow and you play a part.

On April 19, 1995, the newsroom secretary interrupted the morning meeting with a report of an explosion in Oklahoma City. A photographer and I immediately jumped in a car and headed west on the interstate. We thought we would be back by lunch. But the state troopers speeding past us signaled something serious was happening. The city looked like it had been hit by a more familiar tornado and we carefully drove down side streets avoiding broken glass and moving debris. We made it to a parking lot and saw the federal building two blocks away, its façade sheared off and a pile of rubble where the entrance use to be as the 13 floors "pancaked" during the explosion caused by the fuel bomb in the Ryder truck driven by Timothy McVeigh. For 10 days, wearing the same blue suit, I broadcast live morning, noon, and night as survivors were pulled from the pile and the body count ticked up to 168 dead including 19 children in the day care. At one point rescue workers found a tattooed severed leg. It was gruesome and sad. However, it was also inspiring. The workers needed more gloves, more masks, more batteries. The line of reporters bathed in floodlights would turn to our cameras and tell viewers and trucks of gloves and masks and batteries and more would arrive. It was my first experience in direct social work practice.

Then we went into the Red Cross tents and the hospital wards and began telling the survivors' stories, administrators, clerks, and secretaries in wheelchairs and bandages. As the search went on first for a "middle eastern" suspect then the quick capture of McVeigh, parents and grandparents, husbands and wives put flowers and pictures on a makeshift memorial fence and waited for their love ones to be identified. The question remained, why would someone do something like this? And the broader question for me, why do people think what they think, feel what they feel, and do what they do? It was the beginning of my social work education and my journey to private practice. It would take another four years to leave my first dream job and earn my graduate degree. I would return to the Oklahoma City site a year later where the federal building had been levelled and a memorial park planned. But my heart and mind were in a different place with hopes of preventing such tragedies or helping those who survived them.

So my intention here is to explain my thought process and the steps I took in establishing my "practice". After deciding that social work with its broad person-in-environment view was the best fit for me, I had to put on the mantle of social worker, develop a professional identity, and carve out a niche for myself. First, there was the role of social worker in "public" practice as a child welfare worker, and then came trainer, supervisor, therapist, and teacher, the jobs that would pay the bills. In the meantime, in order to run a business, I had to define my product, how to sell it, and what to charge for it. Marketing a service as nebulous as human interaction is like selling space on the internet. Others, like Murray Bowen, Virginia Satir, and Aaron Beck, and more recently Insoo Kim Berg, Daniel Hughes, and Susan Johnson have quantified their interventions. Yet in setting your bicycle apart from bicycles sold by other manufactures, it's necessary to go beyond the fact that yours has two wheels, handle bars, and a seat to distinguishing what sets it apart from other models and why someone should buy and take a ride on yours. To take the metaphor further, are you going to teach them to ride or repair the thing if it breaks down? Most importantly, how will it feel to ride the bike you make? These are all questions that go into developing your unique brand, the professional identity that is you.

Chapter One

Professional Identity

The more than century-old discipline of social work offers a specific identity embodied in the National Association of Social Workers Code of Ethics which includes the values of service, human dignity, and integrity. Social work training articulates skills including reflective listening, open-ended questions, and non-verbal communication. Psychotherapy theorists define interventions like identifying specific behaviors, solutions, and relationship styles. Laws and court decisions require steps like risk assessment, mandated reporting, and documentation. Insurance means diagnosis, informed consent, and billing. These are among the questions to be answered in developing a professional identity. When you decide to "hang out your own shingle", how does all that fit on the sign? Of course, the business sign these days is not a sign at all. And, business is generally not generated by drop-in or drive-by customers. In ten years, despite investing in print advertising, memberships in therapy directories, and direct mail and e-mail marketing, most of my referrals still come by word of mouth from clients themselves.

There are a variety of platforms that serve as the modern day business sign, among them websites, Facebook, Linkedin, and Plaxo, and I use them all. But the one that has been most useful, flexible, and personal is my website: www.michaelajoneslcsw.com. However, it is not having the website that defines my professional identity but the process of developing it. It requires answering and continuing to reflect on the big questions: Who are you? What do you believe? What do you have to offer? How do you think about people and their challenges? How do you work? On what education, knowledge, and experience is your work based? With whom will you work? What will you do or not do? Who are your colleagues and connections? Because this business sign exists in the ether and not at a specific physical address or even on paper it can represent me where ever I work and whatever I do. It holds a space for my professional identity and ideas whether I am in private practice or working for another organization or not at all. It can be changed and updated and refreshed whenever I am.

The process started by reviewing a lot of websites, both those of other therapists and those of other businesses. Then I had to determine the necessary content, like contact information, and nice content, like intake forms and other resources. Most importantly it may be a client's first introduction to me and my services. In that way it provides a first impression and first informed consent, the legal and ethical information required to be provided to clients. This is included in a professional biography, philosophy, and frequently asked questions also contained in the forms clients sign to provide informed consent for treatment and notice of privacy practices. The latter leads to thinking and planning how client information and files, both paper and electronic, will be stored and secured for retrieval until they can legally be destroyed. In my case, it is a locked filing cabinet inside a locked office and password protected software and computer. The first intake forms I used I borrowed directly from the more experienced therapists with whom I worked, changing and updating them to meet my needs as my own experience and training progressed. The forms are therapeutic tools after all, including important background information, symptom checklists, and risk assessments that contribute to treatment. Providing them online was a practical way to save printing costs but also to allow clients to begin to consider the kinds of topics that might be covered in session. Developing a list of resources required me to make connections and to consider what referrals my clients might need from emergency to supportive services. A bibliography suggests options for bibliotherapy.

These days websites are simple to create and maintain by registering a domain name and hiring a hosting company, even designing the site yourself as one of my colleagues did with a Microsoft program. I paid a web designer to pull my ideas together into a cohesive presentation. First, I had to figure out what to call my website. My television handle, Mike Jones, fit nicely on the screen but a quick Google search showed it was already taken by hundreds of others and my business would be difficult to find on the internet. Having my face in the public eye made it easy to put it on my website and business cards. Most of my colleagues do not do this either because they see it as undignified, as if we are selling real estate, or they are simply not as vain as I. But there is a clinical reason I plaster my picture all over my media. Going to therapy, like the doctor and the dentist, it not always easy or comfortable. Many clients are in crisis or distress. In line with trauma-informed care, showing a client who they will meet, where they will meet, and what they can expect reduces anticipatory anxiety. It is really the beginning of the therapeutic process, contemplating change. An explanation of services explains your practice model and socializes a client to the therapeutic process. Answering frequently-asked-questions helps to define professional boundaries. The same rationale applies to including maps, directions, and pictures of the office and building along with parking information and amenities. Including links to blog, Facebook, and Twitter, if not LinkedIn and Plaxo, too, are other ways to extend the reach of a professional identity. This is the mission and vision of a private practice.

Mission and Vision

Change, challenge, pain, and yes, suffering, are as much a part of life as comfort, joy, peace, and triumph. The goal is balance. The source of healing and growth is within each of us individually and with all of us together. My work is not about giving advice or fixing problems so much as joining with you on your journey, to walk a while with you in your search for your new self, your true self, and your place in the world.

Chapter Two

Practice Model

Having established a professional identity, the next step is articulating and operationalizing a practice model, the structure of each session supported by your theoretical orientation in a way that can be explained and documented. It starts with education, training, and practice in the different therapeutic modalities; individual, couple, family, and group, and experience with the multitude of psychotherapy theories. We watch and learn the different intervention strategies; attachment-focused therapy, cognitive-behavioral therapy, motivational interviewing, narrative therapy, play therapy, solution-focused brief treatment, etcetera. We may describe our theoretical orientation as eclectic. However, developing this orientation entails both adopting evidenced-based practices shown to be effective with specific issues and carrying them out with fidelity and embracing practices that feel comfortable in our delivery. This is where your personal learning style comes into play. I do best reading about interventions and putting them into practice. Others are visual learners who like to see the practice modeled. Certification in the delivery of several practice models like Dialectical Behavioral Therapy and Eye Movement Desensitization and Reprocessing require hours of training and supervised practice. This still may not provide a roadmap for each session. Rather than feeling "eclectic" I choose to pick interventions appropriate for the situation with a framework to support the art and science, use of self and personal style that has become my practice model.

Having set the first appointment by telephone or e-mail, and that is the only purpose for which I use either, and directing the client to my website for directions and to complete, print, and bring the initial paperwork, I greet the client in my waiting room with, "Are you here to see Mike?" I learned this from another therapist as a way to protect the client's confidentiality. Similarly, besides being unprotected or unencrypted, telephone and e-mail messages are prone to misinterpretation which I learned the hard way. Clients may find it convenient to let me know what is going on with them and the family which can be very helpful. But my attempts to provide feedback or guidance in a quick written response are too easily misunderstood and instead require the clarification and processing possible only in face-to-face communication. The welcome is followed by an invitation to be seated and a casual conversation about directions, the parking, and restrooms and any other needs like disability access and comfortable seating. For children, in the presence of parents to model, I provide my expectations of their behavior; where they may sit, the volume of their voice, books they may use or not use in the waiting room. I repeat my expectations for their behavior in my office; where they may sit, their tone of voice, what they may use if they ask, and I invite them to take a tour of the office to increase their comfort. This is after I have prepared parents to include their children in subsequent sessions.

The first session allows the client to explain their reasons for seeking service often repeating some of the information they have shared in the initial telephone call scheduling the appointment. I acknowledge the concerns but do not pursue them much further before I have established informed consent and because I do not want the client to disclose sensitive personal concerns before we can establish a safe professional therapeutic relationship, which can lead the client to end therapy before it starts because of strong feelings of vulnerability. Informed consent includes the education, training, experience, and licensure of the provider, an explanation of theoretical orientation, the benefits and risks of therapy, how the client's confidentiality will be protected or breached in the case of mandated reporting and safety risks or limited in the cases of lawsuits against the therapist and collection of fees, how the client may schedule, cancel, and pay for services, and how services may be terminated professionally. The document and the conversation include who may provide consent, how the client may communicate with the therapist, other services that could be adjunct or alternatives to therapy, and grievance and appeal procedures for dealing with complaints and disagreements. Those are the basics.

Articulating these policies takes some thought. For example, I specifically started asking parents whether they are parenting with a partner, and for families of adoption and divorce, who has legal custody of the child client. I ask parents to produce proof of these legal arrangements and for both parents to sign the consent for treatment. Without it I have had to terminate services with a parent and child whose non-custodial parent with legal rights did not consent to the child continuing therapy. Children 12 and older may consent to their own treatment for substance and sexual issues but there are limits to confidentiality here, too. It also saves time to ask clients to determine what kind of mental health benefits they have and whether I am on their specific insurance panel. I have spent too much time on the telephone determining whom to bill or dealing with the denial of claims which calls into question professional and therapeutic boundaries. Putting it in the hands of the client to seek the authorization for treatment and following up on billing is a clinical decision literally requiring clients to buy in to the process. Just like making the initial telephone call, keeping appointments, and showing up on time these are measures of client capabilities and commitment. Clients also make a statement when they fail to show up for appointments, sometimes a statement they are not able or willing to deliver to the therapist in person; the issue is something they can address on their own, the problem is not severe enough to disrupt a busy life, the therapist is not a good fit, another form of help is better.

The rest of the first session is devoted to engagement, assessment, risk assessment, mental status examination, and suggestions for adjunct resources like books, classes, and support groups. Engagement happens as I listen and restate the major concerns of the client, empathizing with challenges and appreciating areas of strength. I take this initial assessment directly from my intake forms which the client has either reviewed or completed. Here I have included questions about pertinent medical and mental health history, previous counseling and psychotropic medications, and developmental and family history. I use a checklist that includes symptoms of depression, anxiety, and other conditions and specific risk assessment questions including substance use, self-harm and aggression toward others, relationship safety, and child, elder, disabled, and animal abuse. I included parent behavioral concerns like stealing, lying, aggression, and manipulation and added a severity scale of 0-10 so the intake assessment also becomes an evaluation tool that can be reviewed as treatment progresses. Having started with an open conversation I use these forms as a tool to cover these specific questions which makes asking them more comfortable and normalizes them as part of the therapeutic process.

Payment is also part of the discussion in the first session. After all, making a living is the point of private practice. Discussing money feels uncomfortable to many, but it too is of clinical concern, part of informed consent. We put a price on our service that says our training and experience has value. The client who sees value in our service is more likely to be committed to the work we do together. We ignore the subject to the detriment of both the client and our own practice. It takes some development of professional identity to say, "I charge $120 for a 45-minute session and I have also agreed to receive insurance payments if you choose to use your benefits." It takes some confidence to provide a bill, wait for a check, or process a credit card payment in the first session right after discussing weighty personal issues. Perhaps it feels like it cheapens the interaction. Instead, it says, "You have just received something of value. You are worth it. I earn my living this way so I can continue to be here for you next week." Discomfort often leads us to ignore the subject to the detriment of the client's treatment and the health of our own business. It says, "What we have done is not a big deal," "Or, I can take care of it later, my client will remember." Often the way clients manage money is diagnostic. Do they forget to pay us and fail to follow through with other commitments? Are they angry with others about money and have difficulty taking responsibility? For us as clinicians, just like clients, money issues can be triggering leading to counter-transference with clients. Can we offer unconditional positive regard if we are not so subtly resentful of the client not paying us? Do we put out the same effort or spend the same time with a client who uses Medicare or Medicaid as one who pays cash? Can I fully be present with a client if I am worried about paying my own bills? The same goes for ethically billing insurance companies by providing accurate dates, times, procedure codes, and diagnoses, and collecting co-pays and no show fees from clients. This continues to take practice as I set boundaries and expectations around payment for services. I will discuss challenges around joining insurance panels in a later chapter.

Informed Consent

"I've been a social worker since 1999, licensed since 2004, in private practice 10 years. I work with individuals, couples, and families, many adopted families since my background is in child welfare. With families I work with parents and children together. And, I focus on relationship, not behavior, except perhaps parent behavior. I consider the parent to be the co-therapist, and I coach parents in addressing concerns with their children. Because of this I do not keep secrets between parties, that is, if a parent or child shares something with me I will use my best professional judgment in determining whether, when, and how to share it with the other people. Specifically, I do not meet with children alone, and children do not have a right to confidentiality separate from their parents. I will tell your child I do not give hugs, we are not friends. I represent this as a professional relationship. They get their hugs from their parents, so handshakes and high-fives with me will do. I do not give or receive gifts. I am not a friend. Friends are the ones who come to your house for dinner. I will not come to your home or school without your consent. If we see each other out in public I will not acknowledge you unless you notice me first. That is to protect your confidentiality. You are welcome to leave me a voicemail or e-mail sharing events or concerns but I will address those questions in session so we can make sure we understand each other. If someone other than you calls me about you I will not acknowledge you as a client. What we talk about in the room stays in the room. I document our sessions to remember what we have done. Some things cannot stay secret. If a child or older person or disabled person or animal is hurt, I have to tell. If someone is going to hurt themselves or someone else, I have to do something about it. I will explain this again with your child. You are welcome to bring other family members into session if you think it will help. If there are others you think it would be helpful for me to talk with such as a psychiatrist or teacher or another therapist, I will ask you to sign a release of information for me to do so. I may consult with other therapists about our work, but I will preserve your confidentiality when I do so. I keep client files for 10 years after we finish our work together then I destroy them. I keep then locked and encrypted. I consider therapy has a beginning, middle, and end. I meet with parents three to four times before bringing the child in and often without the child after we start. It is important to understand the work adults do will benefit the child. You may even decide to spend the session for you. I am not the parent and children are not dry cleaning that can be brought into an office for 45 minutes to have their behavior "cleaned up". I expect to have a friendly relationship with the child but it is OK if they don't like me. I intend to strengthen and reinforce the parent-child relationship so I try to put myself alongside or behind the parent in those interactions. My appointments are 45-minutes long. You may reschedule or cancel with 24-hours' notice. There's a rhythm to therapy. We will work and play in session understanding that play is the work of children. This first meeting allows you to decide whether you feel comfortable enough to continue with me, and I get to decide whether I think I know enough to help. Once we decide we can develop a plan. Sometimes, it takes just a few sessions, sometimes months. I have also worked with families off and on for years as children grow and challenges present themselves. "

Chapter Three

Psychoeducation

Psychoeducation happens throughout the therapeutic process either as information shared with clients or information they have discovered or gathered in their research of their situation. However, I use psychoeducation as an extension of my professional identity, informed consent, and practice model and especially with families and children devote the second session to educating my clients on my theoretical orientation and a more detailed understanding of possible diagnoses. In the second and subsequent sessions, I find it helpful to specifically set aside the first few minutes to hear the questions and concerns of the client since the previous session. That first informed consent meeting is rather intense, full of detailed and sometimes confusing information and full of complicated emotions about expressing concerns to a stranger for the first time. It helps to clarify any miscommunication or misunderstandings. Something a client may have felt uncomfortable sharing the first session might be easier to broach in subsequent sessions. Clients may also come to the conclusion that they are not ready and willing to participate in therapy at the time. And, of course, they may decide that I am not the best fit for them and they want to try another therapist or other interventions and services first. The best reason to set aside time to process is that clients often do a lot of thinking and work between sessions and often come up with excellent insight about the issue and what will work for them. They often return with increased motivation and confidence and willingness to accept coaching and feedback. This client/therapist decision is central to contracting for service.

The second session I usually turn into a trainer, complete with PowerPoint presentation, and explain my conceptualization of the causes of behavior and distressing emotion connecting it with ways to find relief and growth. This is when I start channeling Ainsworth, Berg, Bowlby, Burns, Erikson, Forbes, Hughes, Johnson, Kubler-Ross, Levy, Main, Maslow, Orlans, Perry, Post, Siegel, and Yalom. Because many of my clients are adoptive families, attachment, trauma, grief and loss are the issues. For blended, military, and single-parent families this can also be the case. Even for the rare client, individual, couple, or family, who have not experienced abuse, violence, separation, or substance abuse, real challenges like developmental delays and mental illness impact interpersonal relationships between friends, spouses, and parents and children. It is the impact of trauma on relationships that is the target of my work. Trauma is a big word that encompasses everything from in-utero exposure to violence and removal at birth, to physical injury and multiple caregivers, to natural disaster and war. Trauma affects physiological, psychological, and neurological functioning. It can lead to emotional, cognitive, physical, and social impairment. This often results in maladaptive coping behaviors with potential long term consequences for mental and physical health, interpersonal and social problems, even early death. Because trauma happens in the context of relationships, whether in families or in society relationships are sources of stress and resilience as well as survival and growth. This is a big change in my thinking since graduate school when I railed against a professor who taught "relationship is everything". Like many people I saw changing behavior as the point of therapy. But training and practice has taught me that behavior is driven by basic needs for safety and belonging and meeting those needs is more effective in changing those behaviors.

So, I teach about the brain showing diagrams of the brainstem, limbic system, and cortex. I talk about how the brain reacts to trauma by releasing the stress hormones adrenaline and cortisol with the classic fight/flight/freeze response. I explain that trauma not only primes the brain and body to be super sensitive to stress but also impacts cognitive, emotional, physical, and social development (Perry and Szalavitz, 2006, p. 21-25). Daniel Siegel, M.D. and Mary Hartzell, M.D. (2003) explain how experiences, even the earliest ones, shape memory which affects perception leading to emotion driving communication forming attachment. We grow from the inside out. Because trauma like child abuse, domestic violence, and death most often happens in the context of relationships, attachment and trauma are linked. From experiences we develop coping behaviors, both helpful and unhelpful, and from experiences with parents we develop attachment styles and associated behaviors to cope within the relationship. Ainsworth (1978) and Bowlby (1988) defined four specific child attachment styles: secure, anxious, avoidant, and disorganized. Secure attachment is the result of consistent parenting and results in a child who can self-regulate and has stable self-esteem. Anxious attachment is the result of inconsistent parenting and results in a child who cannot self-regulate and has shaky self-esteem. Avoidant attachment is the result of unresponsive parenting and results in a child who withdraws from control and sees the world as an uncaring place. Disorganized attachment is the result of frightening parenting and results in a child with unpredictable behavior who sees the world as dangerous. Securely attached children are easier to love and teach. Children with anxious, avoidant, or disorganized attachment require more patience and are harder to parent. They are in fight/flight/freeze mode so often that their limbic brain is on alert, their brainstem racing, and their cortex unable to make lasting connections. The goal is to develop safety within the relationship.

The adult attachment style of parents is predictive of the attachment style of their children and is the result of our own childhood experiences (Main, 1985). The adult attachment style influences the way we relate to others particularly partners and children. Mary Main defines four adult attachment styles; secure, dismissive, preoccupied, and disorganized. She has developed an interview protocol to determine attachment style. While I am not trained to conduct the protocol I do ask a series of questions that suggest the adult attachment style of parents. This helps parents develop self-awareness that contributes to effective, mindful parenting and helps me identify parents' specific triggers which lead to reactive rather than responsive parenting.

An adult with a secure attachment style is not someone who experienced no negative childhood events but someone who has processed painful emotions and can help others do the same. A person with a dismissive attachment style may lack empathy for another's pain because they are dismissive of their own, that is, they cannot have empathy for themselves. The person with preoccupied attachment lives in their childhood pain and feels others' behavior including their children's behavior as hurtful. They cannot stay present with someone else's pain without making it personal. The person with disorganized attachment lives in a state of constant anger and fear that makes helping others' with strong feelings very difficult. To be certain the attitudes and behaviors of adults with less than secure attachment are about coping, even if they are dysfunctional or maladaptive. This exploration, while sometimes disturbing and unpleasant can lead to what Main described as "earned security", an integrated self-awareness that contributes to interpersonal connection. It is essential in helping children toward more secure attachment.

Whether working with adults or children, two other topics besides attachment and trauma are important to investigate, developmental history and grief and loss. Conditions like depression, anxiety, trauma, autism, and learning disabilities sometimes result from or lead to missed developmental milestones and loss. Maslow (1943) theorized that survival and safety needs are prerequisite for feelings of love and belonging. A person in survival mode is not free to learn and connect with others. Brain-based conditions like Post Traumatic Stress Disorder and Attention Deficit Hyperactivity Disorder impact the ability to read social and emotional cues. As a result of the presence of a mental illness or the absence of adequate care a person may miss a developmental milestone or get stuck in a developmental conflict (Erikson, 1997). A person who was not able to develop basic trust in a primary caregiver may have difficulty forming intimate relationships as an adult. Whether the condition is organic or the result of experience, it leads to loss. Losses include readily identifiable events like the death of a parent, illness and injury, or more ambiguous less recognized losses like infertility and divorce. Kubler-Ross (1969) calls attention to the specific stages of grieving that are accepted as natural. Identifying unmet basic needs, missed developmental milestones, and unresolved stages of grief help target interventions.

Developing awareness and understanding of attachment and trauma leads to a sometimes uncomfortable realization; traditional parenting and therapy will not help and often hurt. It requires a real shift in parenting, an "unlearning curve" that challenges almost everything we have experienced and been taught about the ways to change behavior and help people heal. If behavior is need-driven, then identifying and meeting the need is the answer not rewarding or punishing behavior. Points and prizes, charts and stars, tokens and timeouts, lecturing and spanking will not work to build or repair a relationship. Fear-based discipline that describes behavior as defiant and oppositional and insists on compliance and respect misses the mark and does more harm than good. Treating attachment trauma, grief and loss, along with neurologic conditions like Autism Spectrum Disorder, Attention Deficit Hyperactivity Disorder, and Post Traumatic Stress Disorder require starting from a place of love and safety. Interventions are counterintuitive and subject to scorn from others who do not understand the specific situation. The tantruming toddler needs more time with Mom or Dad; the aggressive eight-year-old needs more hugs; the screaming teenager needs more play time, and the angry adult needs more care and empathy. (Cue rolling eyes and gaping mouth.) This is where treatment planning begins.

Attachment

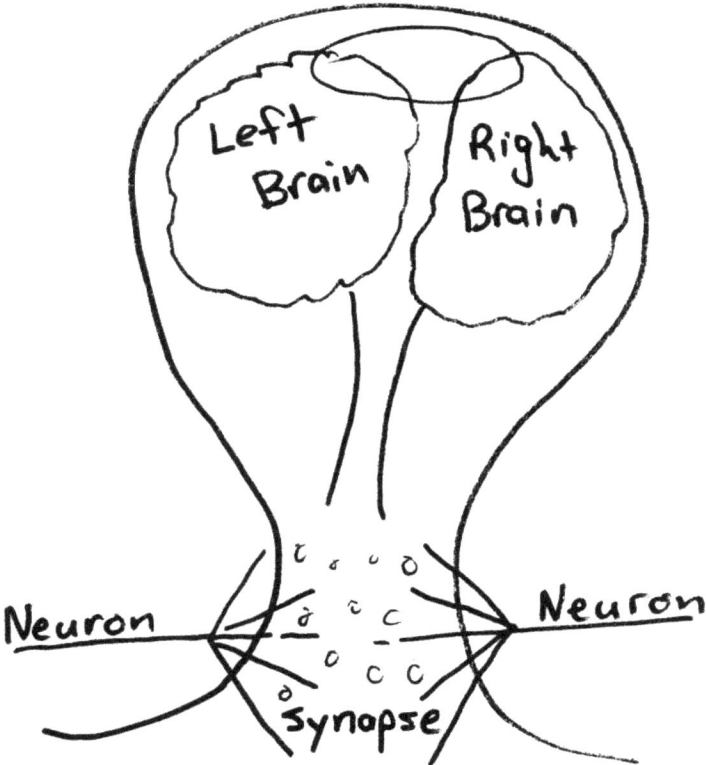

Chapter Four

Adult Attachment Assessment

If the intention of therapy is to change parent behavior in order to increase the child's sense of safety and security, to help them attune to their child and demonstrate it, then understanding what drives the parent is essential to treatment. Identifying the parent's attachment style, understanding their trauma history, and joining in their parenting journey are the keys for me in helping parents help their children heal and grow. Reviewing clients' trauma history and attachment styles also provides context for helping couples and individuals in their relationships whether the issues are communication, finances, and intimacy or grief, mental illness, and substance use. Certainly some issues are best and most quickly addressed with present-focused cognitive-behavioral and future-focused solution focused treatment. But when working with children no one can ignore the impact of early attachment, developmental history, and parenting style to their overall health and functioning. And when working with parents no one can ignore the impact of the way they were parented and their ideas about parenting. Every time I have ignored my better judgment and moved ahead with parent-child treatment without investigating the parents' history and relationship style, the issues have stalled any progress.

Using Mary Main's Adult Attachment Interview as a guide, while certainly not trained or following the protocol, I use a brief set of structured questions that help reveal for me and the client some of the roots of the challenges they have in parenting and relationships in general. The format, order, and tempo of the interview are important. They allow the answers to come unfiltered and unprocessed revealing often unconscious beliefs, feelings, and thoughts that drive present behavior. I say slowly with no additional explanation, "Please give me three adjectives that describe your childhood." Then, I ask for an experience that goes with each of those adjectives, and I wait. I do not explain the question or give examples. Then, I ask the client to describe how their relationship with, first, their mother, and then their father developed from infancy to adulthood and how it may have changed along the way. The follow up question here is, "Did you ever feel separate or rejected by your parent?" Then, "Was there anyone else to whom you felt close; an older sibling, aunt, uncle, grandparent or family friend?" After these questions, I ask about the person's journey to parenthood with some set-up. "From an early age, and for both boys and girls, we usually have ideas about if, when, how we might become parents and what kind of parent we will be." Then I acknowledge that the reality of parenting rarely matches our ideal and ask, "What are your parenting challenges? What do you find most difficult about parenting, or parenting this specific child?" Finally, I ask how the client parent best learns, that is, how I may coach or support them. This has to do with the parent's learning style; audio, visual, or kinetic. "Some people like to read and do, watch and do, or learn by doing." This exchange usually takes 10 to 15 minutes per parent. I conduct the interview with clients in individual sessions and with couples together. Sometimes couples may be hearing this material for the first time in this way, and sometimes one partner will prompt the other with an example. While it may be more accurate to do this interview individually with each member of a couple, the interview is so brief that it does not seem to make much difference. Neither does it seem to make much difference if one or the other partner goes first, giving the other a head start thinking about their answers. It feels more valuable if the client answers, "off the top of their head", or "what comes to mind first", but it is also helpful for partners to hear each other's answers. This self-disclosure and self-reflection often leads to some surprising insights and the beginning of empathy and understanding, which is the whole point.

In terms of interpreting the information from this brief interview, I am listening as much to the depth and tone as to the content and coherence of the answers. The first answer adjectives may include happy, fun, adventurous or sad, lonely, and poor. Based on the adult attachment styles identified by Mary Main, these descriptors are not as important as what comes next. If the examples of childhood experiences are consistent with the adjectives it demonstrates some coherence in the person's understanding of their life story. For example, a lonely childhood in which parents were divorced or absent makes sense, describing it as happy with no further detail does not. I have heard parents describe a painful childhood in which parents were clearly abusive. This does not necessarily predict adult relationship problems. One client reported a happy childhood but with no memories before the age of six. The partner reminded the client that they were ill as a child spending a lot of time in the hospital. The parent seemed disconnected from their own suffering. The couple was asked to care for a boy with anxious attachment, the result of inconsistent care by parents with drug addiction, and a teenage girl with avoidant attachment, the result of multiple foster care placements. The boy was very needy and demanding. The girl seemed independent and wanted nothing to do with adults. One can see that the mother with the dismissive adult attachment style, who could not feel empathy for herself, would have difficulty feeling for these children. You might predict that the mother would find the boy annoying and needing of medication or another placement. On the other hand, she would be unlikely to see the need to reach out to the teenager until it was too late. In the first session, she was most concerned about how to decorate their rooms before their arrival. In contrast another parent reported a sad childhood in which his parents were addicted to alcohol nearly causing a divorce and lots of conflict in the family. The parents subsequently achieved sobriety, the parents and children became closer in adolescence, and the client used therapy to process his childhood. This earned security gave him the ability to be reflective about his own experiences, and his wife's, and thus more likely to be able to be responsive to their children's feelings. Next, the questions about relationships with parents and times of rejection reveal whether the parent experienced acceptance and empathy from their parents, and thus have the ability to provide it to their children. If the parent experienced repair of a disconnection with their parent they are more capable of repairing the inevitable disconnections with their children.

A parent once described an abusive childhood at the hands of her father who she had cut out of her life. It was not the fact that the breach had not be repaired but that the wounds were still very raw, a preoccupied adult attachment style, that made it difficult for this parent to tolerate a child with a disorganized attachment style, his neediness and anger, without taking it personally. To be sure developing secure attachment requires both the anxiety of need and satisfying the need, the rupture and repair of relationship. This is what Daniel Siegel (2013) describes as "the dance of attunement". In the parent-child relationship, the parent leads the dance and has the responsibility to correct the missteps; disconnections can lead to stronger connections if parents have the self-awareness and self-control to make the necessary adjustments. Parents do it all the time when they hear a baby cry and through trial and error find what sooths the infant.

The idea here is that no one gets through life unscathed, without experiences of separation, pain, or trauma. A secure adult attachment style does not mean the parent had a perfect childhood but that they have made sense if not peace with it and so is better able to take responsibility for their triggers when they arise with their children. Children will "push our buttons", but they did not put them there, our parents did. Knowing where our buttons are, and taking care to heal them on our own and take care of ourselves, is essential to mindful parenting. Also, especially in adoption, children have attachment styles that are the result of previous caregivers and experiences, with strange coping behaviors like lying, stealing, and aggression. Adoptive parents can "take themselves off the hook" for creating some of the behaviors, but make the commitment to care for the child. Healing is in their hands. Children do not choose to be abused, and they do not choose to be adopted. Their misbehaviors, intentional as they may seem, are not choices but their attempts to cope with their own triggers. Often the child's trigger is the parent themselves, especially the safe, nurturing parent. This is what Bruce Perry describes as "relational PTSD". The child has difficulty accepting and believing in loving parenting. So, understanding the parents' triggers is as important as understanding the child's.

I do not use this interview to determine the parents' adult attachment styles. That would be unethical, unnecessary, and not particularly helpful. Instead, what is helpful is identifying the parents' triggers so I can notice them and help them manage them in present-day interactions with their children. Is it any wonder that a parent raised by a father with an alcohol problem finds his son's impulsive behavior so difficult to deal with? The father's automatic response is to raise his voice or leave like he did to avoid conflict with his father, both of which disconnect him from his child who needs him close and calm. Knowing this helps him change his reaction to a more effective response. One mother whose adopted son was so anxious that he would not let her go to the bathroom without banging on the door and who once drove away leaving her child at home realized that she used to run away and hide anytime her critical father demanded she do more work on the farm. Knowing this helped her stay and tolerate her discomfort until her son was comfortable that she would not leave him. I keep and refer back to this information often throughout the therapeutic process. Daniel Siegel provides excellent questions for parental self-reflection (2003, p. 133), and I often suggest his entire book, Parenting from the Inside Out, as homework for parents, in addition to a class based on it.

Parents' hopes and dreams about having children, their motivations and reasons for becoming parents, often explain their actions and emotions in facing current challenges. Again, whether we decide to have children or not, to give birth or adopt, and there is huge social pressure do so, each of us has fantasized about the kind of child we would have. Even if for a fleeting moment, we have considered "our" child. Sometimes, that fantasy is fully developed. We decide the gender, we picture hair color, we pick the clothes, the school, the career. Nobody dreams of having a child with challenges. Sometimes, we choose not to parent and a child with challenges shows up anyway. Unplanned pregnancies and grandparents raising grandchildren are two examples. And, the contrast between our expectations and reality often cause conflict, grief and loss. We experience pain and sadness when our children are in pain and we cannot help them, or what we are doing does not seem to be working the way we want. As Kubler-Ross taught us, grief and loss is part of life, a process to be identified and addressed. The last stage she identified, acceptance, is better stated as readjustment. We do not get over loss, we get used to it. We incorporate it into the story of our lives. Grief and loss is a central issue in adoption. Particularly, in adoption, if parents have spent years trying to give birth or considering adoption, they have also spent more time developing a picture of their "ideal child". Usually, adoptive parents are even asked their preferences as to gender, age, and ethnicity, as if ordering at a drive-through restaurant. Even if their "real" child matches their preferences, he or she is not, cannot be, that "ideal child". Not even birth children match up. Each child surprises their parent with their uniqueness, their collection of abilities, personality, and temperament. It is the discrepancy between the ideal and the real that causes the pain. The real child exists. The ideal child never did, except in our minds. Until we grieve, yes bury, the ideal child, it is very difficult to accept the real one. And acceptance is the beginning of attachment and healing. As therapists we are loss managers, we run the funeral home. Acknowledging this and guiding clients through it is part of the treatment plan. Creating rituals can be helpful as an intervention.

In terms of choosing interventions it is very helpful to know the client's learning style. As therapists our shelves are full of books explaining symptoms and diagnoses, exercises and interventions. We learn in different ways, too. A client who can read about their situation brings so much knowledge and understanding into the session for work. There may be little teaching or psycho-education that needs to be done. Some clients take in everything we say and benefit from our explanations and examples. Others really need not just our demonstration of a technique but our coaching in trying it themselves, whether it is using "I statements", tone of voice, or playing with their children. A favorite time was when two beautiful, smart, funny twin boys decided they did not want to follow their mother's instructions to shake my hand and walk out of my office. A loud tantrum ensued, two hours of overturning chairs, dumping the contents of an ottoman, taking the wheels off a table. When their mother pleaded or placated, they cried louder, "You're ruining my life! Let us leave." They could have walked out at any time, they never did. When I got quiet, and coached the mother to stay calm, the chairs went upright, the puppets went back in the box, and the wheels went back on the table with perfect cooperation and skill. Stress created the tantrum, they were testing whether they could trust their mother to hold her ground. Quiet calm created the safety they needed to put their thinking caps back on, and a friendly handshake sealed the deal.

Adult Attachment Interview

1. Give me three adjectives that describe your childhood.
2. Give an example that goes with each of those adjectives.
3. Describe your relationship with your mother and how it changed over time. Did you ever feel separate or rejected?
4. Describe your relationship with your father and how it changed over time. Did you ever feel separate or rejected?
5. Was there anyone else to whom you were close as a child?
6. What were your ideas about becoming a parent and the kind of parent you would be?
7. How do your experiences compare with your expectations? What do you find challenging?
8. How do you best learn? How would you like me to support you?

Chapter Five

Treatment Planning

Depending on the time it takes to provide informed consent, psychoeducation, and assessment, treatment planning may follow in the third or fourth session. Having identified the symptoms of relationship trauma as emotional dysregulation and negative core belief system, established the target of treatment in the relationship between parent and child, it is time to set goals with realistic measurable outcomes and to coach parents to help carry them out. Goals for conditions like anxiety, depression, and trauma may be rather straight forward; rule out illness and injury, refer for medication assessment, identify and manage triggers, develop successful coping skills, and connect to other supports like family and friends. For attachment trauma my goals are to increase secure attachment, increase emotional management, process grief and loss associated with traumatic events, and increase self-esteem or change the core belief system. The difference between traditional treatment and my practice model is the central role of the parent in attuning to the child, providing a safe base, co-regulating the child, helping the child express and process emotions, and creating positive interactions.

First, I like to set parents' expectations for their child's behavior in session. Parents facing the difficulties of their children's sometimes challenging behaviors are anxious to get started, to see improvement, sometimes to have a quick fix. It takes some effort and confidence to stand firm on the preparation of parents to act as co-therapists; to acknowledge their concerns, to teach about attachment trauma, to explain what seem to be counterintuitive interventions, and to convince parents that the time they take to explore their own lives toward self-awareness and self-care pays off with more effective, healing, powerful parenting. Because they want to present their family in the best light, and because they want the therapy to work, they want their child to behave and cooperate, exactly the way they want the child to act at home. The funny part is, most children with attachment trauma can "hold it together" and present themselves well for a while. This ability bothers parents to no end. "Why can't s/he behave like this at home?" "You're not seeing the 'real" child." "He doesn't act this nice at home." "Why don't you come home with us?" The reason is not that the therapist has any extraordinary skill but the therapist is not trying to get close to the child. The therapist is not the parent who loves and cares for them. For traumatized children love and care are frightening to accept, first because they doubt it will continue, and second because they do not believe they deserve it.

That is why I will not work with a child alone while a parent waits in the lobby. What does it say to a child to be dropped off by a parent and to go into a room with a therapist? It says, "You're the problem." And, as Malcolm X asked, "How does it feel to be the problem?" Child trauma is not a child's fault and they should not be expected to fix it themselves. To be sure, important topics may be broached in therapy but the real healing happens in the home; over the breakfast table, on the drive to school, during a walk in the park, while being tucked into bed. The parent is present for those moments and needs the knowledge and skills to recognize and respond to them. For children who do not have a parent who can provide safety, the therapist may be one of the few who does. But the parent who is unable or unwilling to learn to provide safety is the exception, so I attempt to teach them first. I tell the parent I believe them when they report that the child was "out of control" at home. Traumatized children can do some incredibly weird and scary things; hit their brother, hide food, take an I-pod, scream for hours, run away, smoke pot, punch holes in the wall, pull a knife on their mother, burn the house down. And hurt themselves, which they think they deserve. So, helping a child starts with accepting who they are, what they have experienced, and their behavior as an expression of that pain.

I let parents know that when I am interacting with their child I am modeling skills for them to adopt. I will attempt to help the parent and child feel comfortable and welcome in my waiting room and office by letting them know the location of bathrooms and exits, what they may do and use while waiting or participating in therapy, my expectations for their behavior around sitting and talking. But I specifically ask parents not to have expectations for their child's behavior in the therapy room. I do not expect children to sit quietly and listen and answer questions. I do not expect children to like coming to therapy or to show me respect. My goal is to accept the child (and the parents) where they are and to demonstrate safety in the space, which does not and cannot happen immediately. I have had children sit like stone unwilling to talk. I have had children hide behind the furniture. I have had children lash out and throw things at me. All behavior is fodder for the therapeutic process which starts with providing safety and then joining and understanding the underlying beliefs and feelings that drive the behavior. The therapy room needs to be a discipline-free zone. Parents will often "bribe" their child to behave and cooperate in therapy, "a treat if you behave". Nothing could be more counterproductive.

That is not to say I will do nothing if a child or parent behaves in a dangerous or hurtful way. I have had children nearly knock people down racing out of the office, need to be physically restrained by their parents in the waiting room, and ready to run into traffic on a public street. Those are therapeutic encounters, too, requiring everything from de-escalation skills to police back-up. Sometimes people cannot maintain themselves safely even with help in an office and require the structure and supervision of a squad car, jail cell, or hospital room. I model asking for help.

I set a few more boundaries to reinforce the parent-child relationship. I do not hug children or adults or touch them in affectionate ways. Children do need comfort and hugs in my office but I redirect them to their parent, and that is not me. Handshakes and high-fives are just fine. Traumatized children and adults have often been touched in sexual and violent ways, and I do not want to trigger them. And, while I may be a stranger to start, I will not become their friend. Although I try to be friendly, this is a professional relationship. I am not coming to their home like a friend, giving or receiving gifts, or celebrating birthdays and holidays. That is not to say we will not have deeply felt human interactions, but my whole goal is to facilitate those interactions between partners, family members, and parents and children.

I consider the parent to be a co-therapist for their child. To that end psychoeducation, coaching, and modeling is about helping parents be therapeutic, in my office and in their homes. I use Daniel Hughes' acronym PACE or PLACE (Hughes, 2007, p.61) as a guide. PACE stands for playfulness, acceptance, curiosity, and empathy. Playfulness means an attitude of lightness and pleasure in the presence of the child, even in the face of difficult behavior and material. This is not easy to pull off without seeming condescending or cruel but is essential to recapture the innocence of childhood. Acceptance means staying present with the child, behavior and emotions and thoughts all at once, without rushing to correct or judge. We can agree with the feelings and not with the facts, which makes the whole difference. Curiosity requires keeping an open mind, questioning messages and meanings, willing to test theories through trial and error, an interested investigative parent. Empathy means seeing the issue from the child's perspective and joining in their interpretation of their experiences, not imposing our ideas or sympathies. To PACE, one could add L for love or limits, setting safe boundaries for work. A demonstration of commitment to the child, acceptance of their experiences, and joining in their healing are the essential features of attachment therapy. Since the goal is a safe connection to the parent, it does not require correction or teaching, at least not in the moment. This therapeutic stance requires specific behavior from parents; smiling, touching, eye contact, reflective listening, and silence among similar skills. Of course, therapy entails talking but even then, as Daniel Siegel (2003) makes clear, rhythm, timing, tone, and volume are more important than words.

Then, I set a pace for therapy. If parents are the co-therapist, I expect them to be active players, and I do mean play, for play is the work of children, how they process experiences. I try to align myself with parents, sometimes physically, by sitting next to them, behind them, or in a position that supports their interaction with the child, certainly not cutting off the parent or making them only an observer of the activity. I expect to take an active role in modeling PACE while deferring to the parent's role in caring for the child and explaining the family's cultural practices. Parents may bring food, blankets, books, and toys that sooth and support. My goal is balance during sessions, or from one session to the next, of delving into serious material for a while then transitioning into play, going into the trauma then practicing coping skills. For example, I like having parents read books to their children then using the book as a jumping off point for a discussion of the child's specific situation. I also use drawing, games, role play, and storytelling. I often consult with parents alone while the child waits, or check in with parents before bringing in the child. Even this demonstrates that parents are working to change, not the child. Sometimes, parents feel the need to leave the child at home and spend the session on their own concerns. The child benefits here, too. It is important that I join with the parents and that they feel comfortable expressing their concerns, asking questions, and letting me know if they do not understand or do not agree with something I have said or done.

Two techniques I teach parents and use myself I take from the work of Orlans and Levy (2006). First, using statements instead of questions with children and often with adult clients as well. Questions may be the main tool for therapists, but they also put pressure on the client to answer, pressure that often leads to stress, stress that leads to silence or worse, answers that stop the interaction because questions feel intrusive and uncomfortable. Questions sometimes lead to the exact behavior; silence, lies, aggression, that parents describe as defiance and opposition that really say the client does not feel safe. Instead, statements do not require an answer, but allow the client to make a choice; say nothing, agree or disagree with what is said. "Why do you have tantrums when your mother asks you to turn off the television?" does not get you anywhere. Rather, "I think you have tantrums because you don't think your Mom wants you to have fun," is more likely to result in a grunt, a smile, or a "heck yes", that says you have understood and connected. It can be even more powerful to take the pressure off the child entirely by taking them out of the loop and overhear a conversation about them. One four year old who tore up my notes and threw adoption books on the floor hid behind the couch. I asked her parents, "Why do you think the mother gave birth then left the baby at the hospital?" A small voice answered, "I think the baby cried too much." Her statement said everything about her behavior.

Which leads to the second technique, making a statement of the trauma story. Parents and therapists alike want to "start where the client is" and "do no harm". So we work on developing a trusting relationship waiting for the child to reveal their innermost concerns and questions. We wait for the child to be "ready to talk". Most of the time parents take a child's silence about trauma, including adoption, as a sign that they do not think about it. This is usually because the parents do not want to think about it. It does not mean the child does not. And so children and families go for years without addressing major issues while the resulting behaviors and emotions persist. We forget that people, particularly children, do not necessarily talk about their feelings, they act them out. Even in the absence of acting out, children are not likely to share their concerns if they do not understanding why they feel the way they do, or worse, that they will bother or hurt their parents, or be hurt by their parents for speaking up. We acquiesce to this arrangement with our silence. When we say, "We can talk about anything here", but do not specify what, or dance around the subject with subtle hints about "sad and scary" events, we are really saying, "don't tell me, I can't handle it." Loneliness and shame increase. We want to send the opposite message, "We can handle it," and we will not wait and let you to suffer in silence. The trauma statement is firm and straightforward: "We are here to help your parents help you with the fact that you were removed from your biological parents because they did not take care of you, that you spent time in several foster homes, and then had to be adopted." This also helps parents introduce therapy to their child. Instead of, "You are going to therapy because of your behavior," the parent can say, "We have been working with a therapist to become better parents for you. We want you to come with us so we can practice what we have learned."

Attachment Trauma Treatment Plan

Increase secure attachment to parent as evidenced by help seeking and cooperation using attachment therapy, narrative therapy, and play therapy.

Increase emotional intelligence as evidenced by the ability to identify, express, and manage emotions with parent help using play therapy and cognitive behavioral therapy.

Increase core belief system as evidenced by the ability to process grief and loss with parent help with attachment therapy, narrative therapy, and play therapy.

Chapter Six

Family Therapy

Just as with adults, the website can be a good way to orient a child to therapy and the therapist. Pictures of the building, the office, and the therapist give a client an idea of what to expect when they arrive. Some children, particularly adolescents, may feel more comfortable after reading the biography, frequently asked questions, and even the client forms. I try to reinforce the parent role and defer to parents by asking them to introduce their children to me. Then, I welcome the child to my office and explain my expectations for their behavior starting in the waiting room; sitting on the furniture or floor, using an indoor voice, reading and waiting. I do not expect all children to be able to meet my expectations, no more than they can with their parents, but establish my role as an adult who cares for children with an authoritative style. If a child does not meet expectations, then therapy starts right there and then in the waiting room with acceptance and understanding of the client's abilities for self-regulation and feelings about being in a strange place for the first time about to enter into a sometimes intense experience with a stranger. This is not the time for behavior modification or correction. It may also be the first example for parents of the importance of timing interventions. This is not the time for discipline or consequences, in part, because we have not established relationship safety. Instead, it is time to move the brain from emotion to cognition by giving the child a choice, again reinforcing the parent role by having parents practice giving a playful choice, "Do you want to walk in sideways or backwards?" Sometimes, the child cannot tolerate even that much stress, so therapy starts right there in the waiting room as I did once with a smart four year old and her grandparents sitting quietly and chatting for the whole session until she could make a choice to come in.

Once in the room I give the child a "tour" of the room, often giving them permission to take a look at "my" books and toys. I set expectations again about sitting or standing and staying away from my office desk and computer. I demonstrate using a slightly louder voice than the waiting room. And, "You may use my stuff if you ask first. Sometimes the answer will be yes. Sometimes the answer will be no." I ask the child why they have come with their parents, but I do not expect an answer. Rather I want the parents to restate in front of the child that they, the parents, have come for my aid in helping the child or learning to be a happier family. Then, I repeat the same informed consent script I delivered to the parents in the first session, this time showing the child the file I have created with their name and the file cabinet in which I lock it until they are 28 years old. This has the effect of demonstrating serious commitment over time.

I check for the child's understanding and ask for questions. Some children have had previous experiences with therapists, both positive and negative. The informed consent talk often dovetails right into the statement of the problem. "I have worked with many families in which the children were born to their first parents, and there were problems with mental illness or drugs or fighting, and the children had to go into foster care for their safety and sometimes get adopted. And the children are upset and angry and sad about all this, and their feelings come out, like they have tantrums or take food or refuse to do what their parents ask them to do, or break stuff or hurt themselves or their friends. Those are the kinds of kids and families I like to work with." I often make direct reference to the child's specific story and concerning behaviors so that the child knows that their parents and I have been talking about them and there will be no secrets.

Sometimes the child is reluctant or downright refuses to "participate". However, more often than not, if the parents have been coming for several weeks on their own, or the child has been waiting in the lobby while their parents consult with me, they cannot wait to get into the room to see what is going on and to have their say. Sometimes a child is so afraid to stay alone or so anxious to take control of the situation that they will not sit quietly in the lobby. This too is diagnostic and requires either support from another family member or friend to care for the child at home or in the waiting area or frequent timely preventative check-ins with the child. It is sometimes just as concerning when a younger child can sit quietly in a strange waiting room and seem not to be bothered. For this reason, continuing the informed consent, I will check the child's understanding by asking if I am a friend or a stranger to them. More often than not the child will say "friend". Sometimes a child assumes that is the more acceptable answer or they know their parents have been meeting with me for several sessions. But it allows me to clarify my role and our relationship by asking, "Have you ever seen me in your whole life, or have I ever seen you in my whole life?" The answer is usually no, so I say, "So, we are strangers today. Are we going to stay strangers?" Again, the answer is usually no. "Right, we are going to be friendly but we are not going to be friends because friends are the ones who come to your house for dinner or to play, and my office is the only place we will be meeting." This is in addition to the informed consent script repeated with parents and children reinforcing time-limited work.

Because attachment therapy requires the commitment of the parent to caring for the child I like to have the parents identify the child's strengths. This is a powerful start that sets the stage and provides a foundation to return to when we cover more difficult material. I often have the parents draw an outline of the child's hand on paper or their whole body on large butcher paper. Then I ask the parents to state out loud their child's positive characteristics as I write them inside the outline. It may require clarifying that strengths are not positive achievements or behaviors but qualities like intelligence, humor, and kindness. This allows the child to hear in their parents' voice and see in colorful view what makes them special. When there is hurt and conflict at home, these words either do not get said or are easily forgotten by both child and parent. In fact, this strengths-finding activity is important for every client whether an individual identifying their own strengths or a couple naming each other's. Outside the outline I write as parents describe the child's abilities, not what they do well, but what they are attempting; learning to ride a bike, practicing an instrument, or drawing pictures; the positive behaviors that we see on the outside that come from feeling the strengths on the inside. Along the same line, the book, I Love you Stinky Face by Lisa McCourt (1997) emphasizes the parent's commitment to the child which is the starting place for family attachment therapy. After the parent reads it to the child, and if the child is willing, I act out the characters with them playfully; angry alligator, hungry dinosaur, sleepy monster, giving the parent the chance to demonstrate acceptance of the child no matter their behavior just like the parent in the book.

An important side note here is that in therapy I want the parent to read to the child, no matter the age, to emphasize the caregiving role and facilitate nurturing interactions that include sitting close together, use of an engaged and soothing tone of voice, and to recall or redo an important developmental experience. Parents will often have the reflex to have their child read to them, either because the role of teacher is more comfortable or they want their child to learn something from the book by reading it themselves. Sometimes the child is also anxious to read to show that they can or to take charge of the session to achieve safety. This defeats the purpose of the intervention which is to engage the child's emotional right brain in experiencing the pleasure and relaxation of the interaction first so that the information can then be processed by the logical left brain. Once again this mirrors how attachment forms and sets a pattern of joining before teaching.

One intervention that is powerful for traumatized children, particularly adopted children, is narrative therapy. Because story telling is so important both to the relationship and to the parent's and child's understandings of their experiences, I use it throughout the therapeutic process. Parenting with Stories (Nichols, Lacher, May 2002) provides guidance to parents and therapists in constructing stories based on the family's life; establishing a beginning, middle, and end, choosing characters and content, and establishing an atmosphere and setting for telling the story. When I want parents to demonstrate their commitment to the child I start with the claiming narrative. I ask even older children to lie in their parents' laps to listen. Here the story starts before the child was born with the atmosphere and planning for their birth. The parents express their excitement at the pregnancy and preparation for this child. With subtle prompts, they describe the momentous delivery, the celebration of all the family, and all the developmental milestones from the care and feeding of an infant to the first birthday cake in the face. The activity includes baby bottles and blankets in my office. This addresses the child's inevitable curiosity about their beginnings, "Tell me about the day I was born." For adopted and traumatized children the story may be in stark contrast to the actual events surrounding their births, and opens the door to a discussion of their specific facts of life. The storytelling continues with the developmental, trauma, and successful child narratives which often include source material from agency reports, props and other artifacts from the child's life, and the creation of a keepsake scrapbook, art project, or memory box.

Next, I like to emphasize the target of treatment in the relationship between parent and child by having the parent read Patrice Karst's The Invisible String (2000) to the child. The book then becomes a jumping off point for activities. The Invisible String explains attachment connections, so I often use a very visible rope extended between parent and child, the ends tied to each, to illustrate attachment, close in proximity and feeling when parent and children are together physically during happy times, farther away when the pair is separated by distance or disagreement. The parent and child can "tug" on the rope as if to say, "I need you," or "I'm still here." The grown up version would say, "You're yanking my chain," or "I feel the tug of your heart." In moving parent and child together and apart in the room, the rope "accidentally" comes loose, the child becomes "unattached", and the rope falls to the floor. I pick it up in the middle, pitch my voice, and say, "See, this is what we're here to work on, to make sure the string is strong." Then, I reinforce that the real "string" is invisible. The visual stays with children and adults. It also leads to another activity, identifying all of the child's attachment relationships, strong or weak, secure or disrupted. I either cut lengths of string for the parent to tie around the child's wrist or draw a heart with rays extending out to include biological parents, siblings, aunt, uncles, adoptive family members, friends, foster parents, grandparents, and pets, whether living or dead, identified or unknown. The exercise illustrates that a child can have many attachments of varying quality with no competition among them and plenty of room for more. That hits at the loyalty issues adults and children face between biological and adoptive families. It begins to put to rest the very harmful belief that an attachment to the first inhibits the attachment to the second.

Another activity that allows for a restatement of the trauma history and a commitment by the parent to help the child heal is the "hurt heart". I ask the child to draw and cut out a big heart from red construction paper and write their name on it. Then, and this is very important not to have the parent do, I hold the heart and tell the story deliberately, "When you were born you had a perfect heart." I like to hold a doll to represent the child as an infant and often explain that the heart is about the size of our closed fist, holding my hand over my heart, the doll's hand in the same place. The heart, the hand, and the doll are frequent tools. The story continues, "And then stuff started to happen. Your parents started to take methamphetamines and forget to take care of you, and you were hungry." I make a tear in the red paper heart. The child's eyes grow large. "Then, the social workers came and said it wasn't safe for you to stay, and so they took you to a foster home." Another tear. "Then your parents did not come back and you had to meet your new adoptive parents." Rip. Depending on the number of multiple placements and other traumatic events, the paper heart can have a lot of rips. Then very slowly I ask, "Who…will help…you heal…your heart?" And wait. If things are going well, the child may say, "my mom and dad." Sometimes the child says, "I can do it." Often the answer is a confused look. That is when I ask, "Would you consider trusting your parents to help?" I give the torn heart to the child and wait for them to hand it to their parent. Having prepared the parent for this activity I prompt them to list warmly the things they have done, do, or will do to heal the child's heart. Here, it is about the basics; feeding snacks, tucking in bed, taking the child to the doctor, helping with school work, holding them while they cry, playing and laughing, remembering biological and other family members. In the end, the paper heart looks stronger but the hurts are still visible, a metaphor for healing itself. I ask permission to keep the heart in the child's file so that I can pull it out in subsequent sessions to remind us of our work or measure progress along the way.

Sometimes in the first or subsequent session with the child, and before anybody gets too comfortable with the setting, I like to do two not-so-scientific assessment exercises. In the first, I direct a parent and child to face one another, "as if separated by a window" and with mostly facial gestures, some hands, no words, to try to match each other's expressions, first with the parent leading and the child following then with the child leading and the parent following. "Go!" I give them a few seconds to mirror each other as I move around them at a distance observing the result. This can be a playful interaction, quite intimate, sometimes terrifying. When a pair are matching each other well and really enjoying the interaction I get a sense of their comfort with one another, as if you are watching two sweethearts making "goo-goo eyes" at each other. At other times either the parent has difficulty acting so silly or the child finds it so uncomfortable that they look away. If you try it with dyads in a classroom setting you will find how close and comfortable people feel, whether they are friends or strangers. The most disturbing time I had was with a small boy facing his adoptive father who turned and ran behind the curtains and stayed their crying for most of the rest of the session. This kind of closeness felt quite unsafe to that child. The exercise informs what we do next which is usually working on relationship safety through play, starting with teaching parents how to be playful.

The second assessment exercise is parallel drawing. Similar to face mirroring, first the parent then the child leads. I put colored paper on the table, ask parent and child each to choose a colored pencil, direct them to put their pencils on the paper ready to draw next to one another, then say go and wait and watch. I do not give them any instructions about what to draw, how to draw, or whether to talk. I turn the paper over, and with the same instructions, have the child lead and the parent follow. Then, usually silently, parent and child draw. Sometimes the parent will race ahead with a figure or object that is quite well-developed and thought out, but not spoken, while the child struggles to figure out what it is and match it. Sometimes, the child will race ahead etch-a-sketch style while the parent deliberately attempts something more formal. Oftentimes, the drawings will be completely separate matching perfect pictures. Other times, the lines cross and intertwine together. Once in a while, parent and child will draw in the same direction, at the same speed, with a product that flows organically from both, as if a dance has been choreographed on paper. I am looking not just for what the pair produces but how they work together, because the exercise illustrates how they communicate, verbally and non-verbally. When there are two separate forms, it looks like two toddlers doing their own thing side by side but not together. When either one races ahead it looks like one wants to do their own thing but does not care much whether the other comes along. When the result flows it looks like the creation of a comfortable connection. I then take a pencil myself and draw with the child, this time with voice and tone, first communicating what I am drawing slowly so the child can follow along, then asking and waiting for directions so I can follow the child. "I am modeling interactions you can have with your child that say, 'I will go at your speed because I want to be with you', and 'wherever you go I will follow'". Both the face mirroring and the parallel drawing can be good homework for parents to continue at home.

Diagnosis

While accurate diagnosis is an ethical responsibility, many clients see a label as an end in itself as if a pill or other quick fix will cure it. For children and adults, some diagnoses are rather clear cut. Anxiety, attention deficit hyperactivity disorder, autism spectrum disorder, bipolar disorder, depression, obsessive compulsive disorder, post-traumatic stress disorder, and schizophrenia, while complicated especially if co-occurring, have pretty straight forward treatment protocols or evidence-based interventions. Other diagnoses like oppositional defiant disorder, conduct disorder, and reactive attachment disorder are more difficult to identify because their "symptoms" are more subjective. Oppositional to what? Defiant to whom? Reactive to whom? These are individual diagnoses for relational problems that require looking at the whole family. More accurate names for these might be relational traumatic stress or dyadic developmental disorder. The individual diagnosis puts the onus on the person to change when the target of intervention needs to be on the interactions between individuals, particularly parents.

Chapter Seven

Emotional Intelligence

Having established a framework for family therapy and done some initial assessment, it is time to introduce, model, and practice a language of feelings to talk about these issues. It is, after all, the emotional content that distinguishes function from dysfunction, that drives thought and behavior, and that disconnects or connects people in relationship. Here I recall the psycho-education material from the second session, often replaying my training presentation for the child or adolescent to illustrate my point. Then, using Daniel Siegel's hand/brain demonstration (2003, p. 173) I ask parents and children to hold up a hand as I describe the parts of the brain and their roles in physiological functioning, storing pre-conscious emotional memories, and decision making. My hand up flat, pointing to the wrist I start:

"The wrist represents the brainstem, the earliest, oldest part of the brain, responsible for involuntary functions like respiration and temperature, the part that sends our hearts racing and our skin sweating when we are excited or scared. Now fold over your thumb like this. The thumb represents the emotional brain, the limbic brain, also primitive in development, active before birth, and responsible for storing memories of early experiences before our conscious awareness. This is the part that remembers the first time we sat on our bottoms or how it felt to be held and fed, or how it felt when Mom was stressed out about being pregnant, or how it felt to be left alone and hungry. Next, fold your fingers over your thumb. This represents the thinking brain, the cortex, neo-cortex, and pre-frontal lobes that start forming in utero but are not finished until about 25 years old. This is the part of the brain that remembers experiences with words and stories, that learns math and science, that makes decisions about what to do or not to do, most active after the age of four. Now these three parts are connected and communicate

with each other, except when they don't, for example
when we are excited or scared. That's when we
sometimes 'lose our minds' and go into what's called
fight/flight/freeze mode, when we need to fight back
from attack, or run away, or stay still because we are
in danger or think we might be. This is a good thing.
For example, if you are driving down the highway and
somebody almost hits your car, your brain tells you
there's a threat to your life and your body needs to
defend itself. The eyes widen to look around, the
arms and legs get tense to drive the car, and the heart
and lungs start pumping blood and oxygen to make
everything work faster and stronger. You do not stop
to think, 'That guy probably just had a bad day,' no
that part of your brain is not on, you need to save
your life. So, you hit the gas, or you hit the brake, or
you stay right where you are. Then, when the danger
is over you begin to think about what to do, whether
you are hurt, whether the car is damaged, whether to
call the insurance company or the police. Your
thinking brain comes back on. The hard part is that
for some people who have experienced scary things,
even things they can't remember, their brain
disconnects and they go into fight/flight/freeze when
they are excited or scared even when they are not in
any real danger, but think they are. It can happen
often all day long like when a car cuts us off in traffic,
or a teacher raises her voice, or when Dad tells us to
turn off the X-Box. Then, when someone talks to us
we can't hear them because that part of our brain is
not on, and it sounds like Charlie Brown's teacher,
'Wah, wah, wah, wah, wah.' That's what the teacher
means when he says, "Put your thinking caps on."
That's why it's important for us to know and parents
to know when it happens so we can help get our
brains back on. It's also important to know that
sometimes we overreact because our baby brain
remembers when we were alone or hungry and as if
we're going to die. Because, babies can die when they

are alone or hungry. It takes our thinking brain to tell us we're going to be OK. But first the thinking brain has to be on. And, that's what we're going to work on, getting back to calm, so the parts of our brain can work together."

This silent visual then becomes a signal or sign language for when a child or parent feels regulated and calm or dysregulated and upset. Time and time again throughout the process I will ask or the child will volunteer how they are feeling using the hand gesture, sometimes with closed hand indicating they are ready to delve deeper into distressing material, or slightly open hand indicating they need to be nurtured and soothed and it is time to breathe and play. Similarly, I put my closed hands together to represent the left and right parts of the brain, how the left brain is responsible for logical thought and the right brain is responsible for emotional experiences, and how we are going to help the two sides of the brain work together.

The next activity is about developing an emotional vocabulary. I like to start by having parents read their child a book like Today I Feel Silly and Other Moods That Make My Day by the actress Jamie Lee Curtis (1998). I specifically ask the question, "Is it OK to be angry?" The reason is that some parents and people send children and other adults the message, directly or indirectly, that anger is an inappropriate or unacceptable emotion. Nothing could be less helpful. The message of this children's book and all other clinical work, reinforced by therapeutic language and activities, is that all emotions are valid. Identifying, expressing, and managing specific and multiple emotions are essential to healing. And, hearing and validating feelings are essential skills to strengthening relationships including the parent-child relationship. Active or reflective listening does not come automatically or naturally to some, especially those who have never been on the receiving end. A game like Candyland can be a simple start. I call it "Feelings Candyland" and ask parents and children to play together and sometimes I join in to normalize feelings and normalize the expression of emotions so that as we move through difficult experiences we can focus on emotional content. For Feelings Candyland I use the gingerbread men pieces, a die, but no colored cards. I ask the child to give a feeling word to each color on the board from red to green to yellow to purple. I may offer suggestions to make sure we cover the big ones; happy, sad, angry, scared. Often adults are stuck with a limited vocabulary for emotions. A side benefit, although not the most important one, is that I can determine whether the child can count and knows colors in addition to feelings. Then, each participant tosses the die, moves that many spaces, and describes a time when they have that feeling or what makes them have that feeling based on the assigned colors. We play for a few minutes. I sometimes suggest it for family activities. Children often ask to return to the game sometimes with creative sophisticated emotional language.

Another fun theraplay game is Feelings Tic Tac Toe. The grid on plain paper has nine emoji each representing an emotion. The child is encouraged to place an M&M or fish cracker, or if you want to be healthy a carrot coin, on each face and tell when they have that feeling or what makes them have that feeling. The rules are, if they fill up the card, they get to eat the "game pieces" but they may not feed themselves. I take a beat here to wait for the child, and parent, to figure out how this can happen. Often traumatized children feel the need to take control of everything because they do not trust adults to do so, and parents consider that an older child should feed themselves and that feeding an older child seems like coddling them. However, just like the couple at a wedding who feed each other cake, the parent feeding the child is not just an important symbol of their nurturing role but a chance to recreate an early developmental experience. I encourage parents to do it often with food and bottles, baby bottles, juice boxes, or sports drinks, even for much older children, and to make it loving and playful. The same goes for other parent-child activities like reading books, lap rocking, backrubs, combing hair, hide and seek, and wrapping in blankets, as long as it does not trigger the child.

Aristotle provided a good definition of emotional intelligence, "to be angry with the right person and to the right degree and at the right time and for the right purpose, and in the right way." It is difficult for adults let alone children. Scaling emotions is a start. I start by laying out colored paper each with numbers one through five. Using angry and happy as an example, I act out examples from the child's life that would rate anger at level 1, like not getting ice cream for dessert, to moderate anger, 3, like a friend saying something mean, to the highest level 5, a family member getting hurt on purpose. I start quiet with a disappointed facial expression and no body movement, move up to words, "I'm upset" with clenched fists, up to a full loud jumping tantrum, "That's not right!" Parents and children may acknowledge that the child's emotional scale has a default setting of five. Then I ask the child to demonstrate using the emotion happy. Children usually need some guidance from parents to rate the amount of emotion to match the event. Sometimes parents are not comfortable with the extreme levels of emotion children may feel or express in relation to rather serious trauma events like being starved or sexually abused. Often the level of emotion children display over rather mundane issues is really about the traumatic events. Sometimes parents are not comfortable with any but the most urbane expression of emotion. Culture plays a role here, too, what is acceptable in different families. This can keep parents disconnected from their children because they are not able or willing to attune to the child's emotions, many times because they have difficulty acknowledging the depth of the child's trauma. Certainly, parents may display extreme emotion when a child is misbehaving. It takes some coaching to help a parent display extreme emotion over events that seem past for the parent but are very present for the child. This is what I attempt to model.

This activity can be used in two other ways. Having identified several typical life events and acted out the associated feelings, we then talk about the various places in which emotions happen. Then, using the 1-5 scale we talk about in which places different emotional expressions would be acceptable and safe. For example, "it's probably pretty important to stay on a 1 at a restaurant or church, but where would it be OK to go all the way up to a 5?" The child or parent may say, "Nowhere." Most often I suggest a tall mountain, the beach, or the backyard where others are not around. Parents will often suggest the child's room. The point is there must be a safe place, both emotionally and physically, for a child to express extreme emotions, and most beneficially with their parents. Next, I ask the child to stand on the number and color that represents the level of emotion their parents expect most of the time, particularly at home. With back turned toward parents the child will often stand on 1. I send a signal to parents to move the child to 2 or 3 demonstrating that the parent does not expect the child to be perfect and will accept high levels of emotion. The child is often surprised. Then, I ask the child to stand on the 5, and with some cheering from me and parents to really get loud. This is the exact opposite of what parents usually do in trying to shut down an exuberant display. Sometimes predicting a tantrum can take the steam right out of it. In this case, I ask the child to "scale it down" as they continue with an emotion but with reduced energy. It demonstrates that with their brain fully engaged, which is usually not the case during tantrums, and the support and understanding of their parents, a child may have the capacity at least to regulate themselves. Parents are often surprised that a fun and exciting experience can lead to a complete "meltdown" because the child cannot self-regulate. This is an activity I either reference or return to throughout the therapeutic process.

Because emotional intelligence entails more than verbal expression I often use a collection of small percussion instruments from session to session. I demonstrate how each instrument is played then allow family member to experiment with several. In several different formats, I lead with an instrument playing a specific rhythm and then ask each person in the circle to match the rhythm. Each person takes a turn leading. Then I ask parents and children to play the major emotions; happy, sad, angry, scared. No talking is necessary, the emotion is communicated with rhythm, timing, and volume and heard and matched by the others which is the very definition of attunement. We attune and empathize through the use of non-verbal signals more than with language. To help parents and children communicate with each other without the intrusion of language, I ask them to "speak" to one another using the instruments alone. What results is a back and forth "conversation" the theme of which is usually pretty easy to follow. Then the pair explains what they were "saying" to each other, and more often than not their words match their communicated intentions.

Another important emotion that is difficult for children and adults but which is at the core of attachment trauma, especially adoption, is sadness. We must develop an understanding and skills around grief and loss. For this I turn to children's books; Horace (Keller, 1991), Rosie's Family (Rosove, 2001), or other similar stories to open a conversation about sadness. Then I bring out the puppets to tell sad stories. Using puppets takes the focus away from the person and makes expressing sadness safer. Each person in the family chooses a puppet, we go around and introduce them by made-up names, and I start with my puppet telling a simple sad story about a classmate breaking my favorite pencil. By turn, each person uses their puppet to tell a sad story. Almost inevitably, the stories become sadder and sadder and much more real. If not, I go to my "born in a litter, raised on a farm, sold to the city, living with strangers" farm animal story that highlights the themes of separation from parents, siblings, and place of birth. As parents and therapists, we are "loss managers", we have to have a comfort level around grief and loss as if we are "running the funeral home" and know how to guide children through the process, specifically by highlighting events and creating rituals that mark deaths and other transitions. Rituals that include letters to loved ones, poems, songs, pictures, candles, life books, flowers, food, and other memorializing means are excellent in-session activities and homework for families. Throughout therapy we must be alert to sadness and not dismiss or overlook it. For example, a teenager whose biological mother would not apologize for abandoning her fell silent. We could have moved on to school, sports, or other subjects. But noticing the moment and waiting in silence allowed for 45 minutes of comfort and connection between child and parent with cathartic tears releasing years of sadness that had come out in every other way than healing. It was a scene right out of the excellent movie Inside Out (Disney Pixar, 2015) which illustrates the essential role of sadness and all emotion in giving color and context to life. Without sadness we could not gauge happiness. Without emotion life would be rather grey and boring. It is the rainbow of emotion, both heat and light, that makes us human. Emotions are individual and never wrong. Parents and partners can agree with the feelings and not with the facts of a specific situation.

Self-Disclosure

It is quite normal for clients, both adults and children, to ask among other personal questions: "Are you married? Do you have children? Are you a Christian? Are you a veteran?" It is quite human to connect with people through common experiences. And the therapist-client relationship is a human one. However, the questions are professional pitfalls and the answers have serious clinical significance. So, it pays to think through the personal and professional consequences and prepare to answer them. Many in the profession and in the public consider having similar qualities and conditions as clients to be prerequisite to understanding and helping them. Substance abuse treatment and self-help groups like Alcoholics Anonymous and others are contingent on it. It is nearly the first thing a friend or casual acquaintance will offer, "Me too." But for a therapist, the ethical questions are: what are the benefits and risks of self-disclosure and what other interventions could be more helpful and less harmful. It is our responsibility and not the client's to consider this. The answer for me is no self-disclosure beyond the professional education, training, and experience and the perhaps obvious male of a certain age and dress. That does not mean my answer to the questions is, "None of your business." Clients are asking because they want to know if I understand their situation. This goes to the heart of treatment. My answers start with questions, "Why do you ask? (Wait for answer.) Is it important for you to know in order for me to help you?" Then I continue with statements, "These are very good questions. You want to know whether I can understand your situation. The thing is, whether I'm married, have children, etcetera, they are not your marriage or children, and I want to spend our time understanding your unique experience and not imposing my experiences on you. I want to understand things from your perspective. Like all people, we have each experienced some highs and lows in our families, so we have that in common. I know it might seem unfair that I know more about you than you know about me, but I want to learn what your marriage, your children, your faith, etcetera, mean for you. Is that OK?" The fact is we cannot have had all the possible experiences our potential clients have had, and neither should we have to limit our client base to those who have had our similar experiences. That is not to say we might not connect over self-disclosures personal reactions to the weather. Many clients have difficulty setting boundaries; with children, spouses, family members, employers, and friends. Setting this boundary not only reinforces the therapist-client relationship but models for the client how they might do the same for themselves while stopping at the top of the slippery slope to self-aggrandizement.

Chapter Eight

Trauma Therapy

If the purpose of therapy is to support the client in managing the effects of changes and challenges on everyday life then identifying those specific events is necessary. For many people and many problems staying in the present and moving forward will work just fine. For others including children early life experiences have an impact and we ignore this brain science at their peril. Unplanned pregnancy, in utero drug exposure, separation from birth mother, and removal from parents count as much or more than multiple moves and physical or sexual abuse. A family history or other documentation can supply information to construct genograms, timelines, and placement maps. A genogram, like a family tree, identifies multiple generations of family members, the quality of their relationships, and conditions like mental illness and substance abuse. A timeline lays out major developmental milestones along with both major and minor positive and negative events in a person's life. A placement map shows where and with whom a child may have moved and what happened in each home. The process of physically drawing out these on paper is just as important as the finished products. It allows parents to really investigate family life and to focus on details they may have forgotten or wish to deny. In the hearing, the child is educated about important events held in implicit or body memory and validated for experiences held in explicit and verbal memory.

Many parents feel uncomfortable sharing very scary information with children; if the child was a product of rape, if a parent is in prison, if serious mental illness or substance abuse is involved. They fear hurting the child more, they fear dealing with the emotional consequences, they fear the child will adopt the same behaviors, they feel ashamed of the behavior or to be associated with people who make such decisions or hurt their children. I acknowledge all of that to parents. Yet, in most cases, the child is the one associated with "those" people, "that" behavior. The nature of attachment trauma is that abuse and neglect happen in the context of what is supposed to be a nurturing relationship. Humans hurt each other, sometimes on purpose, usually by accident. We are most often hurt by people we count on and love. That is the nature of the work. Parents may take themselves off the hook for hurting the child but they must take responsibility for helping the child heal because children cannot heal on their own. They are also self-centered and egotistical because they are supposed to be. Everything is about them. That means what they don't know, they make up, what they make up is worse than the truth, and what they make up that is worse than the truth is their fault. Children need to be taken off the hook for causing their own trauma. So, children need to know the truth as soon as they are able to handle it, and that is usually at a very young age. Parents of infants and toddlers can practice the story. "You were a very beautiful baby when you were born. You have eyes likes your biological mother. We don't know who your biological father is, but he must have great hair, because you do. But your mother was taking methamphetamines which made her forget about taking care of you. That's why the child welfare worker came and took you to a foster home because you needed bottles and diapers just like every other baby." It is not the details of the story a small child will grasp but the parents' tone in telling it. They may not understand the details, but this story will be repeated for the rest of the child's life as they grow older and ask more questions requiring elaboration. It is their story. It becomes the parents' story as the family grows and acceptance of these facts demonstrates acceptance of the child and those connected to them. If we reject biological parents, we reject the child. Talking about "something bad that happened", "mistakes the parents made", or "they were smoking bad stuff" is a cop-out and damages the trust parents want their children to have in them. Children deserve to hear the whole truth.

Again, a book like The Little Flower (McAndrew, 1999) normalizes traumatic events and the emotions that go with them. After the parent reads the book I have the child draw a flower that represents themselves and then we list the basic needs of flowers and children. It reinforces that the child deserves care. Life events laid out on a timeline provide a roadmap to healing. Both positive and negative developments need to be included: "This is the house where you learned to walk," "this is the house where you ate dry Top Raman because they did not feed you." Sometimes just seeing all of the events lined up on paper is enough to put the pain in perspective; separations, divorces, deaths, moves, and more. Then we use colored pencils to highlight happy, stressful, and neutral events. I ask the client to scale the level of current stress associated with each traumatic event and to prioritize the traumatic events for processing. I do the same for veterans and others with Post-Traumatic Stress Disorder. When we pick a triggering traumatic event we identify the thoughts, emotions, and situations associated with each. We look at the impact on the client's life and what the client is doing to cope, behaviors that are working or not working, normalizing the experience. For example, "if you heard adults fighting at nighttime, no wonder you are scared to go to bed." This is the format for trauma-focused cognitive behavior therapy used with adults as well as children. The client is supported in challenging automatic negative thoughts and cognitive distortions, to learn and practice more effective coping skills, and to develop a narrative of their life that focuses on surviving and thriving. For children it requires the active participation of parents focusing on relational safety, co-regulation of emotion, and intersubjectivity; the ideas that the parent provides acceptance and commitment in the face of difficult experiences and behavior, can manage their own emotions and lend the child support in managing theirs, and can accept the child's interpretation of events while guiding them to mastery of the material.

Role play is an excellent way to bring events to life especially with children because of their interest in fantasy and make believe and their visual learning styles. Role play can be very effective with adults as well. I start by establishing a sense of safety by emphasizing that role play is just that, play, we are playing parts and we can make up the characters and script, which is often empowering to the client. I give the client the power to end the role play if it becomes overwhelming or uncomfortable by practicing a hand signal like "time out" or simply saying, "Mike, can we please stop." For example, adopted children will often like to revisit the court hearing at which the judge decided to terminate parental rights and order the child adopted. In this case, the child plays the judge, the one in charge, and I take the roles of attorney, biological parent, or child welfare worker, depending upon whom the child would like to hear from or "cross examine". The "bailiff" calls the hearing to order, the judge pounds the "gavel", and the witnesses take "the oath" and "the stand". The attorney asks "biological mother or father" why their children were removed and whether they have completed services to fix their problems. The child "judge" will often ask about their living situations and whether they miss the child showing their deep concerns. When the real adoptive parents take "the stand" the attorney asks about their preparation and commitment to adopt. The child "judge" most often asks about food showing their interest in basic needs. The attorney gives a "closing argument" and the judge is asked to decide whether the child will be "adopted". The child acting as judge signs the order along with the parents creating a relationship agreement the child did not make the first time.

The results are sometimes as cathartic when the child wants to talk with a biological family member or even their perpetrator who are not available or safe enough to see in person. This comes after several sessions in which we have developed a safe therapeutic relationship and a practice of emotional expression and soothing coping skills to which to return. Orlans and Levy, (2006) demonstrate this in their trainings. Again, this requires some preparation and set-up, "Remember, you'll really have to use your imagination because I'm pretending to be your bio-mother and I am Mike." The other preparation that makes this intervention more than mastering the trigger event is the role of the parent in demonstrating intersubjectivity with the child. The client is encouraged to ask questions or talk with the "parent or perpetrator". They might even prepare questions or a letter to read. But if they cannot or do not speak, the parent is encouraged to speak for them in "I statements" as the voice of the child which demonstrates they share the child's concerns and interests. At the very least the client's experience is validated. At most we create a moment of connection as when a "biological parent" suggests the child "come to visit" and the child pulls back into the arms of the adoptive parents whom he has seemed to reject. Another time, a five year old boy faced his "uncle" who favored him over his jealous siblings while molesting him. The nonchalant "uncle" asked, "What do you want me to do?" The boy, who had scary tantrums daily in his adoptive home said firmly, "I want you to apologize." The nurturing mother pulled us both out of that most real role play by having us play together again.

When role play is too intrusive and triggering to tolerate, narrative therapy helps people process traumatic life events. Nichols, Lacher, and May (2002) describe constructing narratives that review a child's developmental stages and traumatic experiences. Like bibliotherapy, third party story telling allows the person to take a new perspective on events similar to their own in a way that reduces resistance and dissociation. We heal by hearing stories of people who have overcome problems like our own. With parents children can be engaged in creating characters, plot, challenges, conflict, and resolution which can be empowering and satisfying. I start with a story of a prince or princess who leave their ill parents, the king and queen, on a journey to find a family, going through a scary forest, meeting strange animals, listening to magic birds, until they employ special powers to find a home in which there are rules but also lots of love and care. I ask children with their parents to create their own story in words and pictures. I often provide an outline that includes chapters for the child's birth, traumatic events, moving, settling in, and growing up. Some children enjoy drawing pictures that represent events, others write poems illustrated with drawings. Their reading of their creation validates their experiences and reviewing it over time helps them master their trauma. Similar to the birth narrative I lead parents through telling the child's developmental and trauma narrative placing themselves at pivotal moments to support the child's growth; "and we would hold your hands as you begin to walk", "and if we saw you walking on the street in your diaper we would call the police and get you some clothes and food." Parents often bring props like blankets, bottles, pictures, toys, food, and clothes that bring the stories to life in a way that emphasizes nurturing and safety.

Trauma Metaphors

Psychoeducation in the form of examples, stories, and metaphors can be helpful for children, adolescents, and adults. Two metaphors that may not be scientifically based still help me conceptualize trauma and therapy. First, there is the analogy of airline luggage. Sometimes we carry around a lot of baggage that is heavy and expensive to check. Our whole lives are dumped into the suitcase and it is not particularly organized. In therapy we unpack the big bag, take a look at what is important, get rid of what we do not need, and organize it in a smaller bag that is easier to wheel around and cheaper to carry on. We put it up in the overhead compartment or on the shelf in the closet and we can have access to it whenever we need to recall, refresh, and update the contents. The second metaphor is about the brain as computer. We are working along when we get an error message or everything slows down or stops. Our computer has a virus and files may be infected. The repair opens each document saved on our hard drive, brings it up to the desktop, editing and refreshing, resaving with a new name, organizing documents into the correct file folders, deleting unwanted material, and emptying the recycle bin. Each time we open and look at a file we change it even if the content stays the same. Reviewing thoughts, beliefs, and memories changes them.

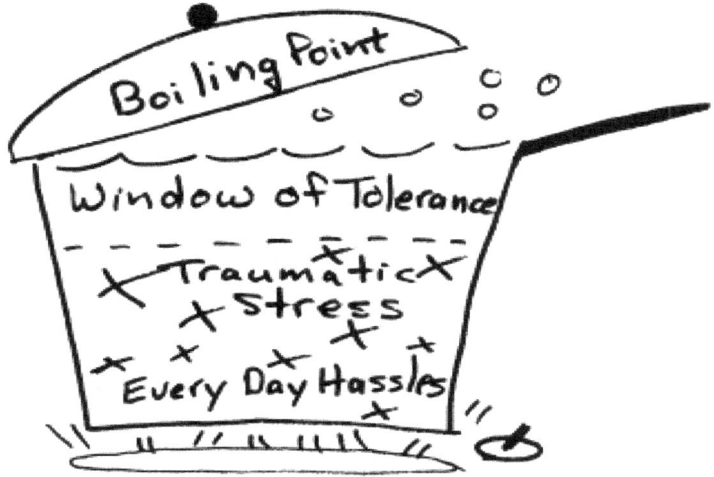

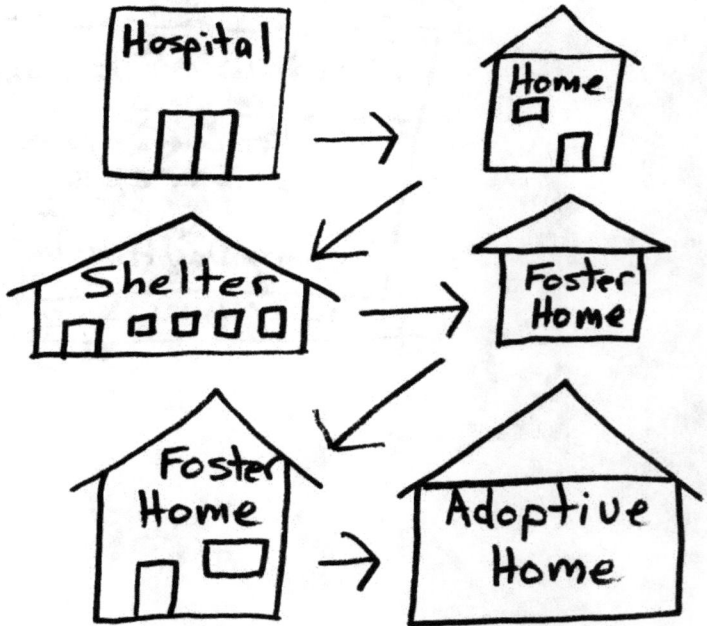

Chapter Nine

Coping Skills

If stress is the body's normal reaction to challenges and changes, then behavior, whether positive or negative, is the person's way of coping with that energy. Sometimes that coping is adaptive, healthy, and legal. Sometimes it is maladaptive, unhealthy, or illegal. Sometimes it is self care. Sometimes it is self harm. We know what is good for us and what is not. The goals are reducing harm and increasing functioning. Having faced those experiences head-on, it is time to return to calm and a sense of safety. This is the pattern or rhythm I try to achieve within a session or from one session to the next. I return to the client's list of strengths and achievements to highlight what is already working. Self-help books and the internet are full of coping strategies; from healthy eating to exercise; journaling to meditation; music to hot showers.

With families and children I introduce these ideas by drawing an "angry volcano". I describe anger as a secondary emotion that we see at the top outside the volcano but below inside, the hot lava holds the primary or deeper emotions. "It looks like anger, but it's really….", and the client, with support, lists frustration, confusion, sadness, illness, embarrassment, and so forth. This is part of developing emotional intelligence, figuring out what we really feel. It also helps the parent or others develop a different response to the client. Rather than reacting to the anger we think we see by misunderstanding, judging, and rejecting, we can respond to the underlying feeling by accepting, empathizing, and connecting. On the sides of the volcano I draw "vents" and explain that while some volcanos "blow their top" destroying people and property including the volcano itself, other active older volcanos never blow their top because they have vents to "let off some steam". Then we list the things the client likes to do to let off steam.

Healthy coping means expressing not suppressing emotions. To that end, I demonstrate and guide children and parents through an exercise designed to discharge emotion. I have used large wet sponges thrown against an outside wall of the building or soft foam balls thrown at the door inside the office. I ask clients to verbalize what makes them angry while throwing the sponge or ball. The physical release and the sound of the sponge hitting the wall are satisfying. I encourage children to "let the anger go" even if the anger seems directed at parents over petty disputes. However, parents need some limits. This is not the time for them to express their anger at their children. Instead, like the role plays parents validate their child's anger, speaking for the child, using "I statements". I connect the trauma history to current emotions by expressing anger for the child about, "leaving my first Mom and Dad", "getting hurt in foster care", "not seeing my brothers and sisters". We return to the activity often, sometimes with children saying they need it, and suggesting it as a regular preventative routine before emotions become overwhelming.

If the goals are building connections and co-regulation then theraplay is an effective intervention. Because parents and children communicate emotionally before they communicate intellectually, theraplay emphasizes the experiential nature of this connection. Theraplay replicates the parent-child relationship across all developmental dimensions; social, emotional, physical, and cognitive. I introduce the four styles of theraplay; structure, challenge, engagement, and nurture. Each allows the parent to introduce an activity and interact with their child playfully in a way that may not be routine in an average family focused on homework, chores, and bedtime. Structure addresses the parent's ability to set safe limits the child can accept. I have the parent measure the child's body; height, arms, legs, ears, and smile. We play a version of "Mother may I?" in which the child is encouraged to jump on one foot, pat their head and rub their stomach, or do jumping jacks until the parent says stop. Challenge allows the parent to set expectations that stimulate the child's development. Parent and child walk across the room holding a pillow between them. The child balances a pillow on their head and walks carefully to dump it on the parent's lap. Engagement fosters social interaction. The parent applies Band-Aids to the child's bumps and bruises or the two create a special handshake. Nurture meets the child's needs for affection. The parent feeds the child a bottle and applies lotion or decorates the child with tin foil. While talking about problems may become overwhelming, theraplay returns the parent-child relationship to playfulness and soothing.

Play and relaxation provide great coping for all clients. For children play is not an escape from problems but a way to make sense of them. Whether they are drawing pictures or making crafts, children almost always reveal themselves. If a parent can learn to interpret the play as the child's language communication and connection happen. Returning to the example of the parallel drawing I encourage parents to be both the leader with theraplay and the follower with creative play by noticing and describing the child's activities as if they are a "play-by-play announcer" or "sports color commentator". Boardgames that include "thinking, feeling, acting" cards or the terrific Ungame provide both the safety of the structure of taking turns and the freedom to express concerns. The magic of The Ungame is that when the session seems to stall the game takes a family back to the very concerns and issues they have come to address, even if it is just the way they communicate and work together. Parenting requires both up regulating and down regulating.   For movement I turn on the music and encourage parents and children to dance or do yoga poses. A collection of small percussion instruments allow parents and children to express their emotions from loud to soft and "speak" to one another with rhythm and sound. I lead parents and children in progressive relaxation. "Stiffen each part of your body starting with your toes and going to your head, making each one like a piece of wood or stone, then go 'soft and floppy'" Parents check the child's body and we repeat. Both children and adults enjoy guided meditation and relaxation breathing either led by me in session or using applications and websites like Calm.com and Franticworld, com.

The Power of Silence

People and parents often feel the need and responsibility to take charge, to lead, and to teach. We most often do so by giving directions and explanations. Talking yields diminishing returns. We help children and partners self-regulate by lending them our self-control. In their anxiety they often draw us in to an endless escalating discussion we feel we must win by repeating ourselves with increasing determination. When we lose our self-control, the anxiety level goes up. When we "lose it" we lose our power. In these situations silence seems weak, as if we are giving in or giving up. It is difficult to realize that doing nothing is doing something; that saying nothing and being truly present speaks volumes. It does not mean we ignore behavior. It means we time our interventions for when our brains are on. Conscious use of silence is a powerful intervention.

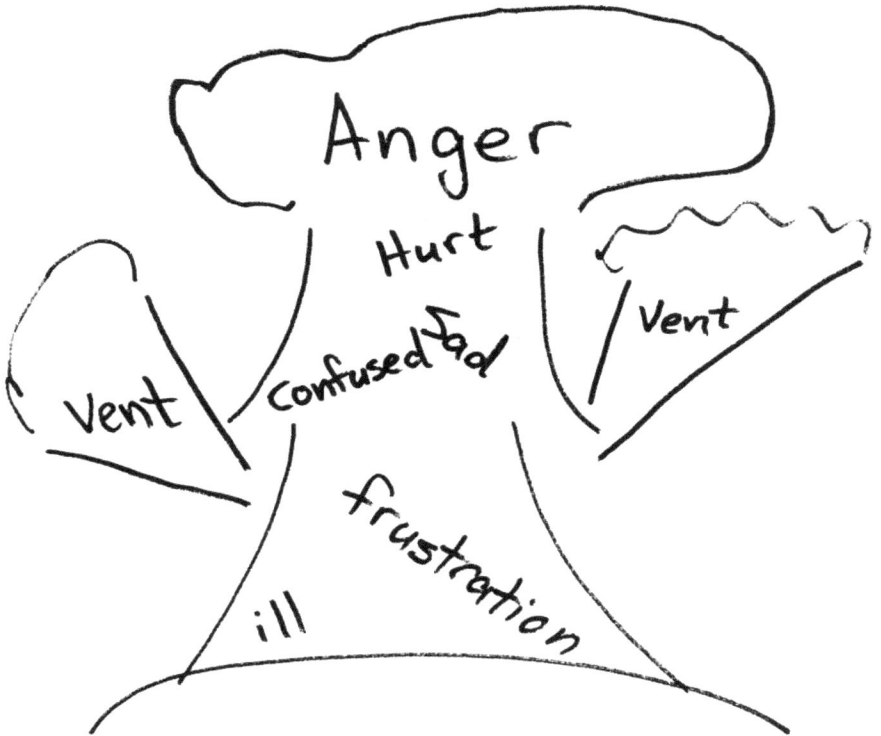

Chapter Ten

Self Esteem

Persistent mental illness, substance addiction, and trauma all negatively impact self-esteem. Whether it is the struggle of overcoming difficult symptoms that limit functioning or facing the unfortunate stigma of a diagnosis, the view of self suffers. This issue ultimately comes up in the ninth or tenth session if not before. Low self-esteem is serious in that it can lead not only to depressed mood but at worst to self-harm including suicide. People with low self-esteem often act in by withdrawing from social interaction or act out by creating conflict with others. Targeting self-esteem starts with assessment. Sometimes adults and children will express how they feel about themselves, "I can't do anything right," "I'm a bad kid." More often the feelings are expressed in behavior and demeanor such as slumping physical posture, downcast eyes, and short stilted speech. One big sign of low self-esteem is the client's inability or refusal to talk about their situation or desire to change the subject. Whether the issue is mental illness or trauma, one common symptom is self-blame thus low self-esteem.

Several interventions can improve self-esteem. The first is naming it and normalizing it. Again, statements are more helpful than questions: "You feel bad about yourself," or "It sounds like you blame yourself for your situation." Because it is a common feeling therapeutic joining is necessary. That means agreeing with the feelings and not with the facts. A return to the initial strengths-finding exercise can remind a client of their positive characteristics. Once a therapeutic relationship is established a continuing attitude of unconditional positive regard and sincere pleasant human interaction set a tone from session to session that helps the client see themselves in a different light. This is why, with families, I do not meet with children alone and, in fact, put the parent in charge of changing in a way that helps the child and the family. I try not to make the child the subject of counseling or the target of intervention in a direct confrontational way. Sometimes people with low self-esteem cannot tolerate hearing positive things about themselves. A compliment or positive remark is likely to be knocked down or dismissed by a person with low self-esteem. The child client and even adults can hear and take in more positive perspectives of themselves if they are delivered indirectly. I encourage parents and partners to focus on and tell positive stories about the client. At home, a parent saying something positive about the child to someone else within their earshot or in a way they will hear indirectly has much more influence and staying power than a compliment delivered directly to the child. The positive statement feels more valid. A good rule of thumb is 10 positive statements for every negative one. This at least will reduce the number of negative comments made about a client if positive statements are hard to find. It does mean we ignore negative behavior but balance the person's experience. Using narrative therapy, parents may construct a "success narrative", a story putting the child in character with talents or "special powers" overcoming obstacles to survive and win. I also use the book Don't Feed the Monster on Tuesdays (Moser, 1991) and role play the child client "talking down" the big monster who spouts negative thoughts as a way of helping the child develop positive self-talk. In this case, it is important not to go lightly but to state the child's worst fears about themselves, "Your birth parents left you because you are too much trouble to love." When the child comes back with, "I am easy to love because my parents do," you have hit pay dirt.

It is imperative to distinguish between a person's self-esteem and their core belief system because they require different kinds of interventions. A person's self-esteem is how they feel about themselves. A person's core belief system is how they see the world. Negative self-esteem is serious but can be corrected. A negative core belief system is more pernicious and less likely to change. For example, a child who is wanted, cared for and celebrated feels they are important, adults are capable, and the world is safe. A child who is rejected, hurt, and shamed feels they are bad, adults are scary, and the world is unsafe. The first child can tolerate failure. The second child expects it. The same goes for adults who have experienced generally positive childhoods and those who have not. Because we behave in ways that confirm our core belief systems, people with a positive view create, find, or interpret situations to fit this picture and people with a negative view do the same. Almost no amount of strengths-finding, compliments, or positive self-talk will overcome a negative core belief system. It requires a paradox intervention. Confronting their negative view of the world with our positive view is counterproductive and will cause the person to dig in and feel unheard. It is like a person who comes home at the end of the day complaining about their work and their spouse either tells them it is not so bad or how to fix it. The person feels unheard, dismissed, and disconnected. Instead, we agree with them and join in their view of themselves and the world. This is very difficult for parents of traumatized children who see as one of their primary roles to raise happy children. What gets in the way is the parents' guilt and shame about the child's trauma and their feelings of responsibility for the child's feelings and the honorable desire to make "the bad stuff" go away or pretend it did not happen. It is not easy, and can be quite aggravating, to be with a person who sees the world so darkly. Parents and other supporters need their own pleasant times and relief valves from the role of helper. This is not the same as depression, but can feel like a bottomless pit of negativity. We have to get down in the muck with the person and not stand on the edge of the hole calling down, "Pull yourself up!"

What this looks like in practice is less talking and more experiencing. That means creating pleasant playful experiences in session and out. Play therapy and theraplay provide both. Taking cues from the initial face mirroring and parallel drawing assessments in the first session with the child, I teach, model, and coach parents to lead the child into play and to follow the child through play. I use multi-colored feathers for parents and children to blow off a table or to work together to keep one feather on the table. I use play dough for a child to create or for parents to "decorate" their child. Tin foil makes great hats, crowns, and bracelets. Lotion can be used to play "slippery hands". Children and parents can create a mirror of their own family or an imagined future using a doll house with figures and furniture. A sand tray provides a contained environment in which a child and parent may create a "world" representing themes from their own lives. Blocks and Lego's, crayons and paint, colored paper and pencils are all media for creative play WITH children. A child or person with a negative core belief system needs help experiencing themselves and the people around them as protective and positive. It is important to know that success in this area can be very fragile. One setback, like a failing grade or the end of a relationship, can send a person back to what seems like square one. Reversing a negative core belief system requires patience and perseverance.

School Focus

Parents want their children to succeed in school. Sometimes, when parents feel ineffective caring for a child with trauma, they focus on an area in which they feel effective, education. They focus on homework, grades, and classroom behavior in a push to help the child succeed at school if not at home. However, the same stress that impacts relationships at home impairs learning at school. And the pressure parents place on school sets back both learning and the sense of safety the child feels at home. Both benefit when parents can prioritize their relationship with the child over school performance. That is not to say that parents should not advocate for appropriate educational services for their children. Heather Forbes (2012) has great ideas to help traumatized children and all children succeed in school. If we provide access to school and a place to do homework, we have done our job. It is the child's education, not the parents'. By giving teachers the job of educating their children and letting go of expectations but not hope parents can focus on the work of building a strong connection with their child that will anchor them during their school days and into adulthood.

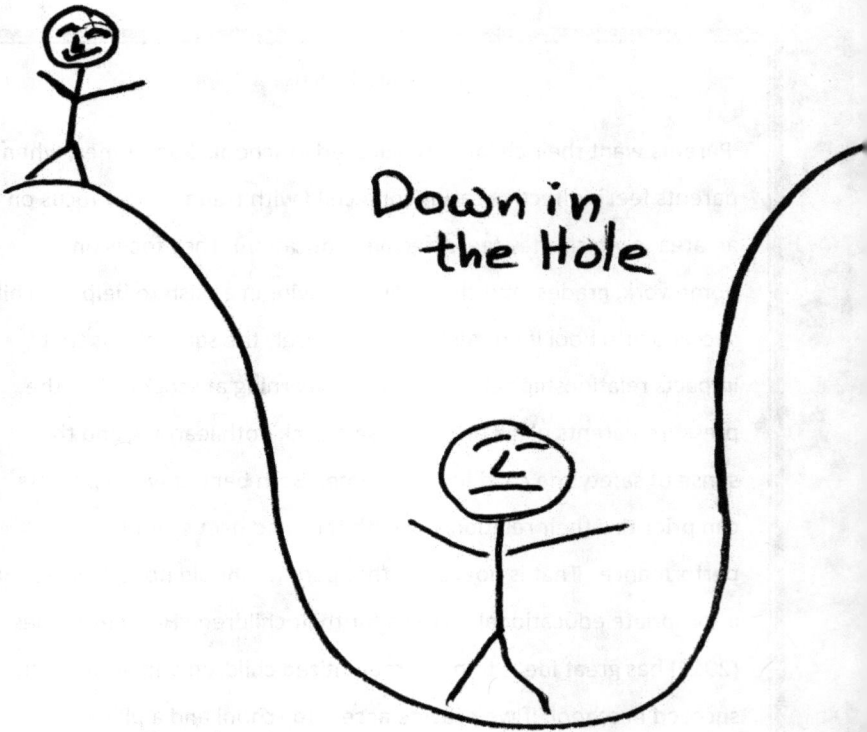

Down in the Hole

Chapter Eleven

Problem Solving

Sometimes the therapeutic process seems stuck. The client sees no progress, and the therapist feels frustrated. The therapist begins to feel the client's hopelessness in facing nagging persistent problems. We feel like blaming the client for not trying. The client feels like blaming us for not helping. We feel stuck together. Sometimes it is about goodness of fit. I may have reached the limits of my knowledge and skills. Another therapist may bring a new perspective, a new start, and new skills to meet the challenge. If, however, we can work through this period together the results can be quite satisfying. After assessment, psychoeducation, and treatment planning, after identifying trauma, expressing emotions, and practicing coping skills and sometime between the first and tenth session specific problem behaviors come to light that require individual attention. Children have difficulty going to sleep and adults have difficulty staying asleep, children take food and adults overeat, and children have tantrums and adults have conflict. These issues are of central concern and deserve to be the focus of work. Some further investigation is in order: What comes before the behavior? What do people do during the behavior? What is the result of the behavior? What has been tried to resolve the behavior? What seems to have worked to reduce the behavior or its impact? What does the client believe about the cause of the behavior? What is the client willing to do to resolve the behavior?

Some attention needs to be given to the understanding of problem behaviors. First, some problem behaviors are symptoms of the condition itself. Problems with functioning; sleeping, eating, elimination, sex, energy, mood, pain, conflict, thinking, socializing are symptoms of diagnoses like depression, anxiety, and traumatic stress. Second, other problem behaviors are attempts at coping with the condition; alcohol, drugs, fighting, isolation, poor hygiene, spending, stealing, and self-harm. Third, other problems are the result of either the condition or attempts to cope with it; employment, financial, social and legal issues. Understanding behavior goes back to beliefs about humans themselves. Interpretations of behavior as good or bad, positive or negative, appropriate or inappropriate, are meant for punishment not for healing. Behavior is need driven. It is either helpful or unhelpful. Behavior is purposeful, but not always for the purpose we think. We do things to increase our pleasure and decrease our pain. The underlying needs according to Maslow (1943) are, and the order is important, survival, safety, love, and belonging. The more sophisticated attachment needs described by Johnson (2008) are safety, attention, value, validation, respect, and love. To these I would add sovereignty, the individual right to one's own body, mind, and spirit. Given this understanding, trying to stop, start, or replace a behavior without looking at underlying needs will have limited success. We must be proactive in meeting the need not reactive in focusing on behavior. The big four behaviors that parents are most concerned about are lying, stealing, aggression, and manipulation. I will take them one at a time.

Lying is a developmental defense that we all use as we grow. A securely attached five year old will lie to avoid the consequences, an eight year old to avoid interrupting their plans, a teenager to avoid letting down parents, and a securely attached adult will not lie because of a well-developed conscience that says, "I am a person who tells the truth." Lying is also a socially acceptable way to avoid hurting people's feelings as when we are asked, "Do I look fat in this?" Or, "How do you like my dinner?" For people with attachment trauma lying is not so much a learned behavior as a defense. Lying to an abusive parent may be a moral imperative. So, telling the truth is about safety. A child, or an adult, tells a lie because it does not feel safe to tell the truth. Their subjective sense of safety in the place, with the person, in the relationship is about perspective. Punishing a traumatized child increases anxiety and jeopardizes safety. The onus is not on the child to tell the truth but on the adult to make themselves safe enough to hear the truth. It starts with not setting up the child to lie by asking questions. The parent who asks, "Did you clean your room?" when they know the answer is no is laying a trap to catch the child in a lie and cannot be trusted. This is not focusing on safety, the first of human needs. If a child or person has developed the habit of lying to figuratively or literally save face, it will take some time to build or repair the relationship. We can be sad about that. We will not be able to believe them. We can practice, "trust but verified." But, we must be ready to hear sometimes harsh "truths" without reacting and rejecting. It does not mean ignoring the facts. If the room is dirty, it needs to be cleaned. When the partner says, "No, I do not like your cooking," the response needs to be, "Thanks for your honesty." Focusing on compliance over connection leads only to more stress for both parties. Prioritizing relationship over power leads to healing.

In the same way, stealing or "taking" is best viewed as a survival skill. If you are in a war zone needing to feed a child, breaking into a store to take food to keep the child alive is the moral thing to do. This is a rather stark example that does not seem to fit with the everyday behavior of a child who hoards food in their room or takes toys, electronics, or cash from friends and parents. In order to address this problem we must take the person's perspective. For an infant or small child, abandonment, hunger, and violence are life-threatening experiences. This trauma is stored in the pre-verbal, pre-conscious amygdala or limbic brain and drives these fight/flight/freeze responses. That is why traumatized children seem to take issues around bathroom habits, eating, sleeping, and transitions to the extremes. The person with a negative core belief system simply does not believe that their needs will be met. They are on their own in the world.

Tackling stealing starts with making sure basic needs are met and doing so in a very dramatic nurturing way. Parents make sure children with food and other neglect issues always have access to food; a designated drawer in the refrigerator full of nutritious food, a stash of non-perishable food in their backpacks and rooms, and frequent snack breaks throughout the day. No locks on refrigerators and cabinets. If it is not meant to be eaten, do not buy it. The same goes for items that are not basic needs. Leaving cash, electronics, and valuables within reach and expecting a traumatized child not to touch them is setting them up to fail, and that is the way they see it. We have no trouble "babyproofing" a home for an infant so why is creating an environment safe from temptation for an older child so different? Expecting a person with sticky fingers to make it through a store without taking something is an unrealistic expectation. When is the last time you left the big box store with only the item you went in for, or only ate the recommended serving size from a bag of chips or quart of ice cream? Can a traumatized child or adult stop stealing? Yes, if they feel that their basic needs will be met, if they feel safe in their home. An older child may not be able to go to a friend's home or to a store or out in public without close supervision. A parent may need to help the child return, replace, or repair the stolen items as restitution using allowance or extra chores. Ultimately, the community may weigh in with arrest, charges, and sentencing the parent needs to support without rescuing the child from the consequences.

The same may be true for aggression especially if it goes beyond verbal assaults and tantrums. We have to acknowledge that our society has a strange attitude toward aggression. We condone it in many areas; in physical discipline, in sports, and in war. Similar to lying and stealing there are times when aggression may be morally necessary to save our lives. This again is often the perspective of traumatized people who have faced truly life-threatening attack in the form of rape and other violence. So, again, while we wish for everyone in the family to feel safe, it is the person who uses aggression who does not. Often, what starts as a minor irritation escalates to complete dysregulation, the person is out of control, they have "lost their mind". Back to the hand/brain demonstration from Siegel (2003), the sympathetic nerve system is activated, releasing adrenaline and cortisol, and the cortex, neo-cortex, and pre-frontal lobes all but shut down. If the brain of a traumatized person is always producing these hormones, and the body's set point for stress is always high, then preventive measures to burn off the excess are necessary in the form of both vigorous exercise and intense soothing practices. We recall the "vents" of the "angry volcano". These are coping skills. They cannot be assigned to the child but need to be lead and shared by the parent. The parent or another adult lends the dysregulated person their self-control. In session, this means teaching, modeling, coaching, and role playing de-escalation skills through the use of reflective listening and therapeutic joining. In practice, it means administering large doses of empathy, to the aggressive person. We check in briefly with the injured party and move quickly to attend to the aggressive child. It does not mean keeping a calm voice. Two year old tantrums require soothing. You take the child out of the situation and sit with them until they settle. The initial non-violent intervention with aggression needs to match the intensity of the situation, "Stop! What's happening here?" followed with controlled, intentional, low, slow language that addresses the emotion and engages the left brain, "You are really upset. I would like us to sit down and talk about this. Would you like to start or do you need my help?" The parent or partner who loses control focusing on blame or broken furniture adds fuel to the fire. It may take back up. In these extreme situations a safety plan is necessary including early warning coping skills, supportive people to engage, hotlines and other resources, up to and including use of emergency services.

As aggravating and frightening as lying, stealing, and aggression, behaviors that seem to be about manipulation can be irritating and exasperating. Children and some adults may talk incessantly to avoid the topic at hand, nag constantly until we give in, go slow or refuse to complete tasks, pretend not to hear what people say to them, or play one parent or sibling against another to find a way between them. It happens at home, and it happens in therapy. It is important not to take it personally because it is not personal. If we understand that anxiety and stress are at play, we can better respond to the seeming manipulative behavior. Like the negative core belief system of traumatized people, their higher baseline stress level never goes away. Both are likely to persist well into adulthood and, without adequate treatment, lead to serious health consequences including heart attack, stroke, and early death. Trauma and its associated adrenaline and cortisol are serious stuff. It can be very difficult to accept that this higher stress level is always present even when the child or adult seems calm and relaxed. The hypervigilance is always there. To cope, the person attempts to take control of almost every situation. We know these people. We may be these people. The "control freak" who needs everything to go their way and in perfect order is a very stressed-out person. Accepting this employs the empathy needed to address it.

A sense of humor helps. After all, manipulation is just good sales, quite a skill. But we do not have to buy. As with the persistent cookie seller outside the grocery store we can politely say no or walk past with a smile until the person learns their pitch will not work with us. It requires extreme patience which is not always possible. However, the opposite reaction simply invites more. That is, when we respond with repeated reminders, pleading, and anger, we increase the anxiety level and the attempts at control continue. Having met basic needs, including affection and play, and set reasonable expectations, we must have the courage of our convictions. We still must be aware of the person's triggers; fear of bath and bed, hunger and pain, isolation and abandonment. In session and out, this is about silently soothing, lending the person our self-control, and remaining consistent and safe. In therapy it means sitting silently for 45 minutes with a child who is bouncing around the room rather than listening to adults, not offering other alternatives to please the child. At home it means pulling to the side of the road immediately when a child begins to act out, not increasing the danger by raising our voices. Children with trauma need adults who are safe and in charge. This is powerful parenting. When we "lose it", we have lost our power and contributed to the child's already high stress level. We have fed the fire. It is not a battle, a test of wills, making parents and children winners and losers. It is the difference between authoritarian, permissive, and authoritative parenting styles. The authoritarian rules by fear, increasing anxiety, impairing relationship. The permissive parent gives in early to avoid an unhappy child only to wind up with an unhappy teenager who cannot be satisfied by anything. Either situation is out of control and can become downright dangerous. The authoritative parent leads with confidence, able to admit mistakes and make mid-course corrections, offering children consultation and experiences in which to learn and grow.

As Daniel Hughes (2007) suggests, when problem behaviors become the focus more structure and supervision may be required. About the time we think we have all the routine and watchfulness we can stand, we probably need more. At this point, if not before, I offer parents my family chart (Appendix) with suggestions on how to organize the family's schedule, needs, expectations, privileges, and consequences. It may seem excessive to schedule every part of a family's day from sun up to bedtime but it provides the kind of predictability that reduces anxiety and increases safety, just as it does in the military and in residential treatment centers. Traumatized people do best with routine. Think about running a bed and breakfast or cruise ship. Both vacations start with clear orientations about the schedule, what is available to guests, what is off limits, what will cost extra, when meals are served, what services are offered, what to do in case of emergency. Can you imagine what would happen if this information was not provided? This kind of clear instruction allows the operation to run more smoothly. The family chart makes for a good agenda item at regular family meetings.

As to a schedule, if one hour intervals leaves too much free unstructured time, then shorter timeframes may be needed. Then, I place a major focus on meeting the needs of the members of the family with affection and play being at the top of the list followed by food, clothes, bed, hygiene, school, doctor, dentist. Affection and play with parents, hugs and high fives, tossing a ball and board games, are essential to building attachment which provides the connection for parents to direct and teach children. Basic needs do not include bags of chips, dessert, telephones, television, sleepovers, and shopping trips. Now the expectations are meant for all members of the family, not just children. The list should be achievable, positive, and short; everybody stays safe, do chores, return what you borrow, attend family meetings, accept no for an answer. Avoid words like respect and manners, they are subjective. Be specific, describe what you want to see, "use please, thank you, excuse me, I'm sorry"; "knock before entering, dress for dinner, hats are worn outside only". As opposed to taking away privileges, every day starts with no privileges and parents provide privileges as they see expectations met. Privileges include electronics, sleep overs, shopping trips, and amusement parks. Children can live until adulthood with no privileges at all and receive only what they can handle. To make this work consistently, minimize reminders and the word no. The child asks, "May I watch TV?" The parent answers, "Yes, as soon as your room is clean." When handing out privileges it is a big mistake to say yes. Instead, "You may watch your show", or "You may watch for 30 minutes." If the child cannot turn off the television, the parent does not remind but does not hand out the privilege the next day.

Now to consequences, discipline is about teaching not punishment. We expect children (and ourselves) to miss the mark. The message needs to be, "Mistakes are welcome here." Teaching takes the form of natural consequences, do overs, and making amends. Some mistakes or poor choices require empathy and no consequences at all. If a child breaks their toy by carelessness or on purpose say, "You must be sad about that," but do not blame or ridicule the child with, "That's what happens when you are reckless with your stuff. Do you know how much that costs?" No, do not replace it, let experience teach. There are a few choices, per Daniel Hughes (2007), when a child does not meet expectations. 1. Ignore it because the child has had a bad day. 2. Do it for them because you love them. 3. Have the child pay someone else to do it. 4. Award privileges only when it is done. Finally, when a child has hurt someone by word or deed, help them make it up to the person in a concrete way, and award privileges only when it is done. You make brownies with the school bully to give to his classmates. In another example, a mother empathized with a boy whose trauma tantrums at bedtime led to his kicking a hole in the closet door. She did not berate him. She gave him the telephone to call the home store. He used adult language to order a new door and helped the handyman install it. He did the math. It cost him 20 weeks allowance. He learned he could fix his problems and felt great about it. His mother demonstrated her commitment to him while not damaging the relationship.

When these behaviors persist despite parents' commitment to non-traditional parenting, I pull out Daniel Hughes' (2007) hearts and walls exercise in session. I deliberately draw a stick figure of the child as an infant as I tell their story, "You were born with a perfect healthy heart, and then stuff started to happen." Then, I draw a figure of the child at the age at which they were abused with a heart with some dark marks. "Your parents were having problems with mental illness and drugs, and they did not feed you, hug you, and watch you." Arrows pointing at the heart indicate the abuse and neglect. Then, I draw a figure of the child at the age at which they were adopted or when the behaviors started to appear, this time with a box around the heart labeled "yelling", "tantrums", "taking food", "ignoring adults" and arrows pointing at the heart labeled, "love", "play", "safety", "hugs". "You are a smart kid and you learned how to protect your heart by putting up walls. Sometimes the walls keep out the good stuff." Lastly, I draw a figure of the child as an adult with a healed heart and question marks where the walls might be. Over several sessions I bring these drawings back, next roleplaying the child talking with themselves at different ages. One parent plays the child as an infant. Another parent portrays the child at the age they were hurt. The child plays themselves as an adult. Very importantly, I play the child with the defensive behaviors defending them as necessary because "you cannot trust adult to take care of you" and "you should keep the walls up when we're grown up." The parents are able to identify with the innocent infant and to empathize with the abused child. The child is also able to see themselves and their parents from different perspectives. I end with a lingering question, "When do you think you'll feel safe enough to let down the walls and let the good stuff in?" Having taken time with this exercise, the child will usually say something like, "When I'm 8", or after their next birthday. Sometimes they say they will trust their parents when they are teenagers or as adults, but the seeds of change are planted, a positive future is in view.

Emergency Services

Sometimes a parent simply cannot keep the child, themselves, and others safe without engaging emergency services including police, hospital, and residential care. But taking these extreme measures can be risky for the future of the relationship. The way in which parents ask for and explain the assistance can make all the difference. First, we do not call the police, hospitalize a child, or place them in care because we cannot handle them and have given up and need others to parent them or to punish them for their behavior. That is a cliff from which it is difficult to step back. We literally employ the services of law enforcement, hospital staff, and residential caregivers to help us keep the child and others safe. Second, it is a mistake to believe that anything but first aid is being offered to stabilize the situation and to offer parents respite and space to regroup. Then, having separated the child from the family it makes a repeat more possible in the minds of the child and the parents thus increasing traumatic stress while parents are attempting to repair the rupture.

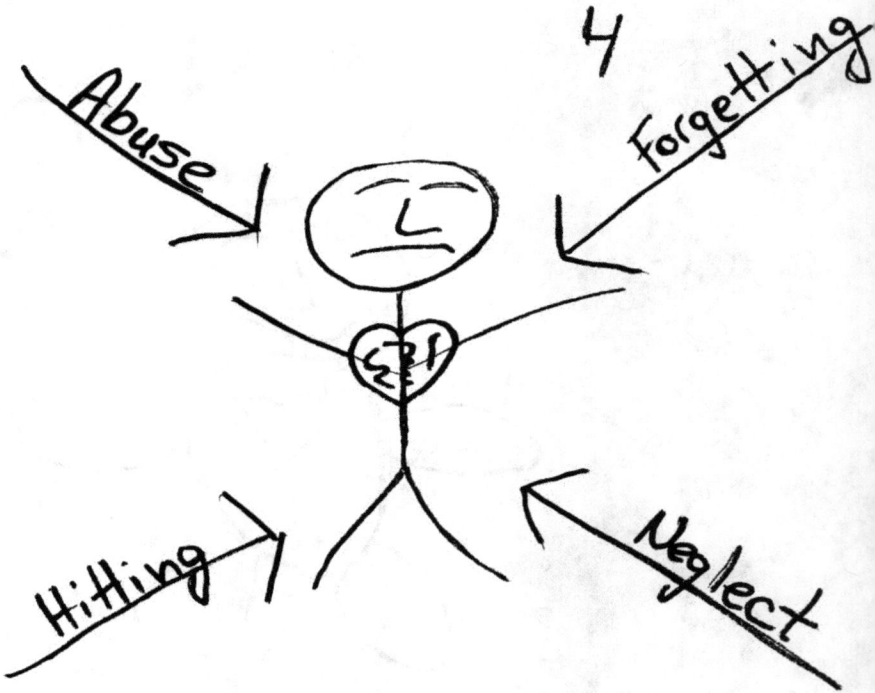

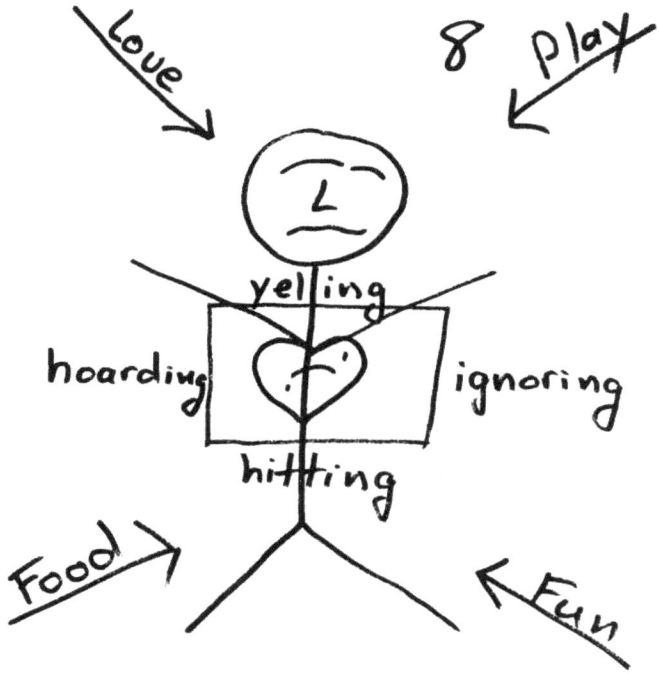

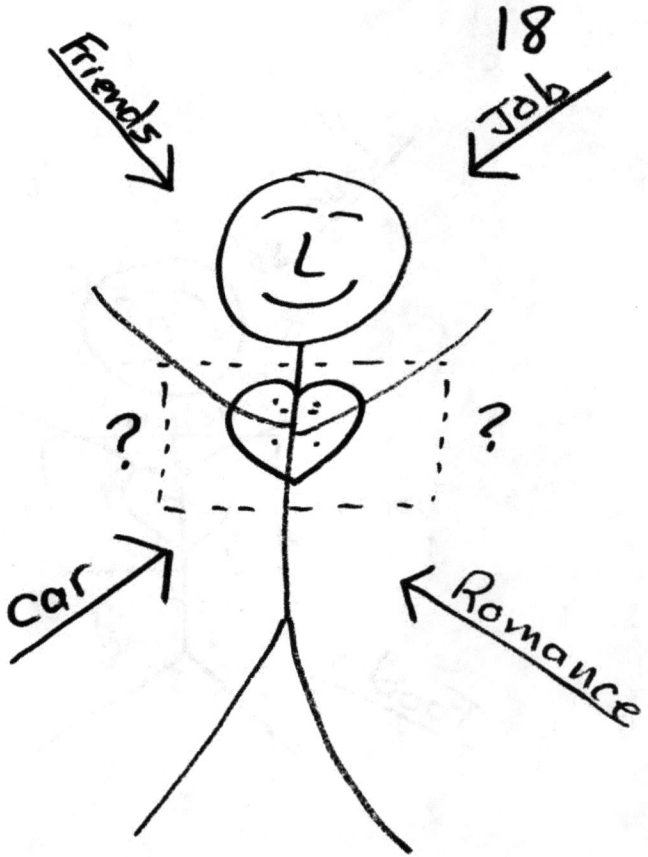

Chapter Twelve

Evaluation and Termination

Every session could be the last session, so every session encompasses some elements of evaluation and termination. Right from the first session I remind clients that based on my professional philosophy and practice model therapy has a beginning, middle, and end. The evaluation process is not just part of every session but the essential intervention of therapy itself. What is working? What is not working? What have you tried? What would you like to try? How can I help? In addition to following a specific treatment plan that includes exploring trauma, practicing coping skills, and increasing emotional management, I often start each session with, "What would you like to work on today?" or "What would make this session worthwhile?" The idea that we are always measuring progress in a time-limited process brings energy, motivation, and urgency to therapy, just as assignments, tests, grades, and a semester end bring focus to a class or course.

Each of the following questions has a purpose as an intervention in and of itself. What have we accomplished? In the daily struggle of life and the routine of weekly sessions, clients sometimes do not see how much has changed since they started. I return to the initial assessment paperwork, the client's description of their concerns, and the scores they gave specific symptoms. It is often surprising and gratifying for the client to hear, "Your child's tantrums have decreased from daily to rare. How did that happen?" What is left to do? Having resolved their most critical and persistent concerns, clients will often turn to higher functioning desires or, having experienced success in smaller ways are now ready to tackle more serious problems. How might that be accomplished? If clients have learned new skills, like communication, they may feel more competent to try resolving issues on their own or in another format, like group therapy. If the client has seen little or no improvement in their situation, the answer may be to change the treatment plan, change the therapist, or try again at a later date.

The process of therapy is often more important than the content. The understanding, knowledge, and skills clients learn in session are applicable to many life challenges. The purpose of therapy is at least two fold, to address current concerns and teach skills to apply to future issues. The skills I try to teach and model are empathic and reflective listening, keeping boundaries and setting limits, and problem solving that respects individuals and relationships. What has worked? The question is meant to prompt the client to identify the specific skills and interventions, to consolidate the gains from the therapeutic process. What has not worked? This question is just as important as clients assemble a toolbox of life skills. The two questions posed together illustrate the very practice of problem-solving; identifying issues, listing possibilities, evaluating options, making choices, trying solutions, measuring progress.

Evaluating the therapist is not just about rating their work or collecting success stories. What worked with the therapist? This question invites the client to give the therapist feedback. Giving feedback is another communication skill clients may use in the future. What did not work with the therapist? The client gets the chance to provide perhaps critical feedback in a positive way, yet another skill applicable to life in general. More specifically, these questions put the client in the empowering position of being the customer of a service. They ask the client to consider the nature of that service and what works for them. In a parallel process, the client learns how to solve their problems and how to shop for services to help them in the future. The questions allow the therapist to adjust the treatment plan and interventions if the client keeps them engaged or to make a referral if the client decides to hire another service provider.

Having participated in the therapeutic process the client may have uneven progress in the future and experience setbacks both simple and serious. What are anticipated challenges? This question helps clients expect, normalize, and prepare for such challenges. In the case of mental illness, substance abuse, and trauma, there are stressors, triggers, and relapses. For couples and parents, families enter different life cycles and children grow into subsequent developmental stages. Issues like adoption and learning disabilities are life-long. When to return or seek help? Clients often seek therapy when they are in crisis or when everything else they have tried to solve their problems has not seemed to work. This question helps clients specify what circumstances would warrant returning to therapy to avoid a crisis. A person with mental illness may want to return if they have had a major loss like a death in the family. A person who relapses on drugs or alcohol may need a quick intervention. A couple may return before they decide to adopt or have another child. An adoption family may want to return as the child becomes an adolescent. I specifically encourage parents and children to return when things are going well to celebrate success normalizing therapy as a support to well-functioning families.

Because the client-therapist relationship continues in perpetuity after services have ended, it is important to restate the legal and ethical requirements at least during the last session. I nearly repeat everything I said during the first session with parents and the first session with children. "I will always have the responsibility to protect your confidentiality because we will always have only this professional relationship. That means I will still not acknowledge you in public or do other kinds of business with you. For example, I will not be attending your family weddings and you will not be attending my funeral." My responsibility for protecting the client's privilege and privacy does not end with the termination of services. I keep files and records for 10 years after the end of services or until the child turns 28 years old. If I have not heard from the client for 30 days I send a discharge letter offering further services or a referral to another therapist informing them that I will be closing their file to officially end my responsibility for their care.

Because my practice philosophy is based on the social work value and ethical principle of the importance of human relationships, I try to spend some time in each session and particularly in the closing session to honor my relationship with the client. The client, whether individual, couple, or family, has taken a chance to share very personal information, to open themselves to examination, and to try news ways of interacting. They have made themselves vulnerable in an intimate relationship that is by its nature unequal, the therapist has more power and does not reveal themselves in the same way that clients do. It makes the therapist more responsible. That is why it requires a license and continuing education, consultation, supervision, and audit, and is subject to complaint, investigation, administrative sanction, and legal action. At the very least I express my appreciation of the relationship acknowledging what we have done together. Further, especially with children and families, marking endings is an important therapeutic intervention. For clients, especially children, who have experienced abrupt changes as a result of their trauma; removal from biological family, moves from one foster home to another, little or no contact with important family members, closure is necessary. For this, ritual is important. This can include recalling shared memories; the fun, human, personal, silly moments, blowing bubbles, drawing pictures, playing games in therapy. Returning routinely to a book, game, or toy in session may seem repetitive as if we are making no progress and should be focusing on something new. However, these rituals are as important to the therapeutic process as they are to family life. Of course, I encourage clients and families to return to therapy if crises, changes, or new challenges arise, but I also encourage clients, especially traumatized and adoptive clients, to return when things are going well. This is also a therapeutic intervention to consolidate and celebrate gains and to reset the role of the therapist from rescue to support. Especially with children, even adolescents and adults, I like to end the final "see you later" session by reading Dr. Seuss's Oh The Places You Will Go! (1990), which has a realistic message predicting a positive future. Reading it models and reinforces the nurturing and positive relationship.

Sticking Points

Particularly with families, and especially adopted families, when healing seems to stall four issues are most likely to be at the root. Adult trauma: parents have not dealt with their own childhood experiences and they are being triggered in ways that keep them from being warm, nurturing, and consistent with their children. This often requires putting the family work aside to address the parents' issues either in consultation or with outside therapy. Adult relationships: parents have deep unaddressed difficulties in their relationship, differences in their ideas about parenting, and inability or unwillingness to communicate about them. This requires stopping conjoint parent-child work to avoid further damage to focus on these issues. Adoption attitudes: due to unresolved infertility issues that make adoption seem shameful, parents are unable to appreciate, communicate, and facilitate relationships with biological family to benefit their children and family. Theoretical differences: the client, despite adequate psychoeducation, cannot accept and does not agree with a relationship-based non-behavioral orientation.

Chapter Thirteen

Nuts and Bolts

Office: I looked for office space that would be centrally located, convenient, and comfortable for my clients and me. I first joined a group of therapists already in practice and received great guidance and support. I signed a lease that I could afford even with the ebb and flow of income and expenses that make private practice require a careful budget. The office needed only to be big enough for a desk, some furniture, filing cabinets, and therapy supplies with utilities, heating, cooling, and housekeeping included. I learned in changing offices that location is more important to me and my budget than to clients, as clients will come from all areas if they are satisfied with my services. Another consideration is that office leases may increase in cost from year to year and that keeping office space in a group setting means finding and maintaining relationships with colleagues to share the space. My specific office has a separate locking entrance so that I can have any office hours I choose. I have subleased my office to colleagues for times when I am not open both to help pay the rent and to develop relationships with colleagues who might someday share building space. Many therapists use offices in or near their homes. I prefer to keep firm physical and psychological boundaries between my professional and personal lives to avoid real or perceived conflicts of interests and to provide space for self-care.

Office Hours: When I first started in private practice I was concerned about having enough clients and being available at times convenient to them. I soon learned that an eight hour day full of appointments was not sustainable either by energy or competence. First, I determined that I could reasonably serve six clients per day, and I do not mind taking appointments back to back. Second, I determined that clients will come to appointments on a schedule convenient to me. Third, as I have changed office hours to meet other responsibilities, adjusting clients to new appointment schedules and times was not particularly disruptive. Once I set my office hours I have learned to be firm with that boundary for my own convenience and to set limits with clients.

Telephone: Having set strict boundaries between professional and private life, between home and office, I set up a separate office telephone, a wireless business line, with an easy to remember number.

Voice Mail: My voice mail outgoing message says, "You have reached Michael A. Jones, LCSW. Please leave your name, a brief message, and your telephone number, even if you think I already have it, and I will return your call as soon as possible. If this is an emergency, please hang up and dial 911. If this is a mental health crisis, please call the San Diego Access and Crisis Line at 1-888-724-7240." I check my voice mail only during business hours and usually only once or twice a day. It is password protected. I am usually able to return calls within 24 hours. I return them with a message once and do not send appointment reminders to clients. I am not available 24/7 and for emergencies, thus the message needs to include the other emergency numbers. I change my voicemail message when I am out of the office for more than two or three days with, "I will be out of the office and returning on (date)." I do not say why I am out or where I am going. If I have a personal emergency, I check my voicemail remotely and ask a colleague to return calls. If I need to invoke my professional will my trustee would change my voicemail to indicate my absence, return calls, contact all clients, and make referrals to other therapists.

Computer: A simple laptop computer has been all that is necessary to run my private practice. It has enough memory and applications to run accounting and billing applications, with internet and e-mail access for extra expense, and able to drive a projector and speakers, also portable, for use in trainings on the road or occasional work from home. The computer and everything on the computer is password protected, backed up to two external hard drives on a regular basis, and locked away when I am not in the office. When I needed to update my computer, setting up and moving files to a new computer was relatively easy. The computer also drives a separate scanner and printer.

Website: I determined that my website would be my business sign. I contracted with Network Solutions to register my domain and host my website as well as e-mail for a relatively affordable annual price. I contracted with a professional designer to create my website design even though colleagues have done a very good job on their own using website design software. I decided on www.michaelajoneslcsw.com , although unwieldy to repeatedly spell out, because it says everything, is unique to me, and unlikely to be repeated.

Facebook: I set up a separate professional Facebook page to establish my private practice on that platform, to stay connected with colleagues, to send out notices about my business, to promote my work, and to stay current in the field. My web designer created my Facebook page. I check my page daily, try to post pictures and comments as often as possible, and respond to friends whenever appropriate. It takes a conscious effort to continue to try to collect friends.

Twitter: Although I rarely use it, it seemed like a good idea to set up a Twitter account with MAJonesLCSW. I rarely post anything and rarely read other tweets.

LinkedIn: I posted a profile on LinkedIn long before my private practice then updated it to match the style of my website and Facebook page. Rather than staying connected with colleagues, LinkedIn is a way to stay connected with potential employees and employers.

Praxo: I set up a profile but have never checked or used it.

Billing Programs: I started with EZClaim and have updated it twice in ten years. It creates client accounts quickly and simply, allows me to create and print paper billing claims, to record payments for each client, loads a template for progress notes, and allows me to write and save the latest progress note. EZClaims and other billing programs also have online versions. So far I have not connected my billing program with my accounting program or online programs.

Accounting Program: I started with Intuit Quickbooks to record income and expenses. I hired a professional accountant to set up a detailed list of accounts. I moved to an online program with a small monthly fee five years into my practice. I have never connected my Quickbooks to my bank accounts. I produce annual reports that work very well for taxes.

Banking: Similar to the separation I created between home and office, personal and private telephone, I started the same way with banking. But because the business banking fees were so high, and because I have not incorporated, I make deposits and make payments from one personal account.

Taxes: I hire a tax preparation firm to complete my federal and state taxes for about $500 per year. Unlike a typical job in which one or two W-2 forms are enough to complete taxes online, private practice, even as a sole proprietor, entails multiple W-2 and W-1099 income statements, self-reported cash income without statements, and detailed expense and depreciation deductions. The firm provides guidance for paying estimated taxes and funding retirement accounts.

Retirement Accounts: I have typical 401K or 401B retirement accounts with a few W-2 employers. But since starting private practice I have rolled over all previous retirement accounts into a Traditional IRA and fund a Roth IRA and a SEP IRA based on current tax laws.

E-mail: I decided on askmike@michaelajoneslcsw.com to connect my e-mail to my website through one hosting company, Network Solutions. I was also trying to be catchy and to distinguish myself from other businesses. The cost is included in my hosting package. I put my e-mail address on my website and business cards. As time goes on it seems e-mail may be necessary but less useful. It is still the primary professional communication forum for sending and receiving contracts and referrals, encrypted client information and forms, receiving notices from major organizations, and to connect with insurance companies. Some clients like to communicate by e-mail but as I learned early on I now make it clear that I only communicate by e-mail about appointments and not about issues and problems that require careful consideration and clarification only possible in session.

Business Cards: I created my business card to match my website and Facebook page, to include my picture and as much contact information as possible. Business cards seem sort of de rigueur as a touchstone for interpersonal connect. I have also used them as a written reminder to clients of our next appointment. But as time goes on and clients begin to use their smart phones the business card has become a way of steering clients and other professionals to that platform.

Facsimile: Just like e-mail and business cards, a fax machine and number are becoming less necessary and less useful. I share one fax number with an office of other therapists. When encryption is not possible, it is another safer way aside from snail mail, to send and receive confidential information. Online and cloud-based formats will soon make facsimile obsolete.

Scanner: I finally bought a scanner for two reasons; first, to try slowly to turn my hard copy files into electronic files for ease of use and to save paper and physical file space for long term storage. I also need to scan some files to upload to insurance websites.

Credit Cards: The business credit card came with the business checking account. It may not be necessary but it seemed like a good idea to separate business expenses from personal purchases, to access business discounts, and to provide a record of expenses for tax purposes. Some vendors such as retail and wholesale stores, airlines, and licensing agencies prefer credit cards.

Forms: I borrowed or stole my intake, assessment, and documentation forms from colleagues at the start, then began to adjust them based on my needs and trainings. I adjusted my intake Client Information form to include information valuable to me; referral sources, e-mail contacts, and expanding a symptoms checklist to include scaling questions. Federico Grosso's training (2009) was very helpful in updating my Informed Consent and Confidentiality Agreement, Notice of Privacy Practices, Authorization for Release/Exchange of Information, and Policies and Procedures.

Progress Notes: I started with a simple progress notes template then updated with the help of the Federico Grosso training (2009) and insurance company policies, trainings, and audits. (Appendix)

License: I applied for the California associate social worker certificate with the Department of Consumer Affairs Board of Behavioral Sciences in 2000 and started supervision toward licensure soon after. I was lucky enough to receive supervision for free while employed at Child Welfare Services. I shared study material with other social workers studying for the licensing examination and purchased an on-line practice examination which helped greatly in preparing for the examination. I earned my LCSW license in 2004. Maintaining the license means a renewal fee of $118 every two years.

Continuing Education: I have been lucky enough to receive continuing education toward licensure as part of my employment and as a result of teaching courses. I have paid for additional individual trainings and conferences when I found the material helpful to my practice. The cost of continuing education is tax deductible. While I extensive experience and specialties in several areas I have decided not to pursue advanced certification in any particular intervention.

Business Tax: I learned a little after starting my private practice that a sole proprietorship is also a business requiring paying the $35 annual San Diego City Business Tax. It is easy to register the business and to update the certificate annually at the City of San Diego website.

Business Insurance: Just like homeowners or renters insurance, business insurance at about $40 per month covers any damage or losses of computer, telephone, and furniture due to accident, fire, and theft at the office. Cleaning services do have access to my office, and I have had one attempted break-in. Insurance does not preclude needing to encrypt and double lock client files, but it does demonstrate my efforts to protect client privacy in the case of a breach.

Malpractice Insurance: Necessary for an active practice, with $1 million/$5 million coverage for individual and maximum claims, I pay $212 per year to Allied World Insurance Company. The National Association of Social Workers has also started its own malpractice insurance company now in competition with Allied World.

Insurance Panels: While some therapists never take insurance payments and accept cash paying clients only, I decided to try to be available to as many clients as possible by applying to join all the major insurance panels and several Employee Assistance Program panels. At the start the application process was time consuming and several major panels were not accepting any more providers in my zip code. The process became more streamlined with the use of the CAQH clearinghouse in which you update your information for insurance companies to check. As time goes on, insurance companies close or merge, change names and addresses, and it is nearly impossible to determine how to join a new insurance panel or whether I am a provider. Also, the mental health benefits under the major insurance companies are often subcontracted and the details as to authorization and payment are completely different for each policy holder. So, I simply ask each client to check with their insurance company and their specific mental health benefits to determine whether I am on the panel, to get pre-authorization as necessary, what payments and co-payments will be, and to whom I am expected to submit claims.

Professional Organizations: I have been a member of the National Association of Social Workers since 2003. It used to be a requirement for purchase of my malpractice insurance. There are many business and professional organizations recruiting therapists as members. This is a matter of personal taste. I maintain my NASW membership because it represents my professional identity. There are additional benefits, from discounts to insurance to training.

Insurance Billing: If all the above is correct billing insurance companies for my services is relatively easy. My EZClaim billing program prints claims on the Health Insurance Claim Form 1500, available in bulk at the office supply store or on line at FilerX.com. I set aside a few minutes at the end of each week to print, sign, and mail claims. Each insurance company has a different billing cycle, from one week to 60 days, thus irregular income that requires budgeting. Most insurance companies will send an explanation of benefits with payment or denial explaining what needs to be done in terms of correcting information to have the claim approved and paid. Most often it is something simple such as an incorrect birthdate or diagnosis code. But if the client or I have not done the up-front work to determine the accurate mental health benefits provider, authorization requirements, and approved diagnoses, payment may be in jeopardy along with the treatment and client-therapist relationship. It requires diligent follow through.

Electronic Billing: Most insurance companies offer online claims submission. Once you create an online account submitting claims and receiving payments electronically is easy.

Electronic Files: Aside from Microsoft documents such as professional letters and forms, spreadsheets and presentations that do not require password protection I have yet to purchase the online software to go "paperless" to protect Personal Health Information in accordance with the Health Insurance Portability and Protection Act. This is a rather expensive and labor intensive endeavor but a worthwhile goal to create new files and begin to scan old ones.

Paper Files: I have hundreds of client files that require HIPPA protection for years to come. They require storage in a locked filing cabinet in a locked office and space is an issue. After ten years I am beginning the process of destroying client files that are past the California state requirement of seven years and the general practice standard of ten years of storage.

Furniture: Because I work with couples and families who need to be able to sit closely together, a "love seat" works just fine without inviting people to lie down on a long couch. A couple of other chairs allow for a family to participate together. A big coffee table with storage doubles as a crafts table. A desk and chair and filing cabinets are enough for an office. A couple of chairs that looked cool are not because children twist and turn and fall off of them. A bookcase and shelves hold all my supplies. I bought it all second hand. Diplomas and licenses provide full disclosure. I painted my own wall art for fun and to save money, abstract pictures that allow my clients to see in them what they want to see without imposing ideas or meaning.

Filing Cabinets: I found huge filing cabinets second hand and ten years later they are completely full of files that need to be stored another ten years. It is time to join the new millennium and move to cloud storage that meets HIPPA requirements.

Books: The Diagnostic and Statistical Manual of Mental Disorders is mostly mandatory. The rest of my clinical library (See Bibliography) I have collected along the way by interest or training. I suggest many books to clients as psycho-education or an extension of therapy. I have learned not to loan my books because I have lost several that way. I use many children's books in therapy with children and families. This collection continues to grow as I find books about specific subjects but I continue to depend on the same basic texts I use to facilitate parent-child interaction and as a jumping off point for therapeutic activities and games.

Games: The therapy websites and conventions are full of board games and card games meant for use in therapy. I continue to go back to Candyland for use in developing emotional language and to the Ungame for use in practicing reflective listening. However, I have learned that almost any game can be "therapeutic", and I do not need a big collection to be effective.

Toys: Some toys seem essential for working with families and children; dolls, puppets, and blocks. In my excitement at starting private practice I collected musical instruments, a doll house, and sand tray but find that I seldom use them and return to simple paper and pencil.

Supplies: Colored paper, colored pencils, crayons, and markers are my major therapy supplies. Office supplies like printer paper, envelopes, pencils, pens, and a good calendar and planner are really all that is necessary. Printer toner and postage stamps are occasional expenses.

Professional Will: As we are responsible for our clients' confidentiality, privacy, and records even after our retirement, injury, or death, someone has to take charge of our practice if we cannot. As part of my estate planning, I included a professional will in my trust documents and designated by trustee to work with a trusted colleague to contact my clients, offer services or referrals, complete billing and documentation, arrange for storage and destruction of files, and to maintain my practice until my return or to close it upon my death if I have not done so already.

Epilogue

Lessons Learned

I have learned a few things about running a business and providing counseling, supervision, and training over ten years, and I expect to learn a lot more in the years ahead. I expect never to achieve expert status, only competence. That is why they do not call it private "perfect".

- In an attempt to build my private practice I joined several therapy directories, purchased advertising in various media, attended many professional forums to distribute business cards and brochures, and sent out e-mail appeals to referral sources. Most of these investments had no returns. I still receive most of my referrals from existing clients, attendants at my trainings, and directly from insurance companies.

- As a social worker and therapist it is sometimes difficult to ask for and talk about money and payments. However, in terms of professional practice it is unethical not to. I have learned to make sure up front that I will be paid for each and every session. I cannot stay in business providing services for free and allowing a client balance to grow interferes with therapy and results in lost income that cannot always be written off.

- My practice model for working with parents and children includes an assessment of the parents' trauma history and attachment styles. Sometimes, when parents are in a hurry to see results, when they seem "too nice and normal" to ask, or when the child is in crisis, I have moved forward with family therapy. Every time I have gone against my better judgment, it has come back to haunt me and to stall progress. It becomes a sticking point I cannot ignore and must address, which I could have known up front.

- While I would like to be on the cutting edge of new media with the use of texting, e-mail, and online counseling, it just does not work for me. I have no desire to be constantly available to clients by texting. I started with openness to e-mailing with clients but I quickly learned the hard way that I can misinterpret what a client is asking and clients have misinterpreted my comments in response. So, while clients may feel the need to explain themselves in detail in an e-mail, I have learned to respond only in person so that I can clarify the client's concerns and check and correct any misunderstandings. Now, I tell clients I can make, change, and cancel appointments by e-mail and that I will read client e-mail, but that I will not respond by e-mail but only in person during our next session.

- Sometimes, you just have to apologize for making mistakes or for not being able to help. Therapists are human, too. Despite consultation and supervision, sometimes personal issues interfere and cause a break or disconnection with a client. It is therapeutic to own it and apologize. It can even propel the process forward. Other times, in an effort to be helpful I have accepted clients I could not help and needed to send them on to another therapist. The quicker I can figure that out and make the appropriate referral, the better.

- To that end, while, at first, I was anxious to have clients and schedule appointments, I have learned that it saves a lot of time and frustration to conduct a more comprehensive intake interview over the telephone or even an initial consultation before scheduling a first session. Some of the questions I need to answer during the intake: who is the client and is that person willing to participate. Sometimes a spouse or parent will try to make an appointment for an adult who is not seeking therapy on their own. If the client is a child, who has physical and legal custody, who will participate with the child in therapy, who has the legal right to consent to treatment with the child. I have had step parents and grandparents seek therapy for children for whom they do not have custody or legal rights. Finally, is the issue or concern something for which I have training and experience.

- When I started I was intent on being as open and helpful to clients as possible. And, so I would tolerate clients for therapy and supervision not keeping appointments, cancelling at the last minute, and showing up late. I rescheduled them time and again, even calling and reminding clients to make and keep appointments. Then, I decided I needed to keep better boundaries in this regard. And, so now I do not call clients to remind them or follow up after no shows, do not reschedule clients after two no shows, and collect no show fees before scheduling any more appointments.

Bibliography

Ainsworth, Mary D. Salter, Blehar, Mary C., Waters, Everett, Wall, Sally N. (1978) Patterns of Attachment: A Psychological Study of the Strange Situation, Psychology Press, New York, New York.

American Psychiatric Association. (2013) Diagnostic and Statistical Manual of Mental Disorders, Fifth Edition, American Psychiatric Publishing, Washington, D.C.

Berg, Insoo Kim and Dolan, Yvonne. (2001) Tales of Solutions: A collection of Hope-inspiring Stories, W.W. Norton and Company, New York, New York.

Bowlby, J. (1988) A Secure Base: Parent-child attachment and healthy human development.
New York: Basic Books

Curran, Linda A., BCPC, LPC, CCDP, CAC-D. (2013) 101 Trauma-Informed Interventions: Activities, Exercises and Assignments to Move the Client and Therapy Forward, PESI Publishing and Media, Eau Claire, Wisconsin.

Curtis, Jamie Lee. (1998) Today I Feel Silly and Other Moods That Make My Day, Joanna Cotler Books, Harper Collins Publishers, New York, New York.

Danziger, Paula. (2004) Barfburger Baby, I Was Here First, G. P. Putnam's Sons, New York, New York.

Dickson, Donald T. (1998) Confidentiality and Privacy in Social Work A Guide to the Law for Practitioners and Students, The Free Press, New York, New York.

Erikson, Erik H. and Erikson, Joan M. (1997) The Life Cycle Completed, Rikan Enterprises Ltd., New York, New York.

Forbes, Heather T., LCSW. (2012) Help for Billy: A Beyond Consequences Approach to Helping Challenging Children in the Classroom, Beyond Consequences Institute, LLC, Orlando, Florida.

Forbes, Heather T., LCSW and Post, B. Bryan, LCSW. (2006) Beyond Consequences, Logic, and Control: A Love-Based Approach to Helping Children with Severe Behaviors, Beyond Consequences Institute, LLC, Orlando, Florida.

Grosso, Federico C. (2009) Advanced Applications of Law and Ethics for California Clinical Social Workers.

Grosso, Federico C. (2008) Managing High-Risk Clients: Protecting the Mental Health Clinician.

Hughes, Daniel A. Ph.D. (2007) Attachment-Focused Family Therapy, W.W. Norton & Company, New York, New York.

Hughes, Daniel A., Ph.D. (1998) Building the Bonds of Attachment: Awakening Love in Deeply Troubled Children, Rowman & Littlefield Publishers, Inc., Oxford, England.

Hughes, Daniel A., Ph.D. (2004) Facilitating Developmental Attachment: The Road to Emotional Recovery and Behavioral Change in Foster and Adopted Children, Rowman and Littlefield Publishers, Inc., Oxford, England.

Houston-Vega, Mary Kay, Nuehring, Elane M. and Daguio, Elizabeth. (1997) Prudent Practice: A Guide for Managing Malpractice Risk, NASW Press, Washington, D.C.

Johnson, Sue Ph.D. (2008) Hold Me Tight: Seven Conversations for a Lifetime of Love,

Kaplan, George C. and Main, Mary. (1985) The Adult Attachment Interview, Unpublished Manuscript, University of California at Berkeley.

Karst, Patrice. (2000) The Invisible String, DeVorss Publications, Camarillo, California.

Keck, Gregory C., Ph.D. and Kupecky, Regina M., LSW (1995) Adopting the Hurt Child: Hope for Families with Special Needs Kids, A Guide for Parents and Professionals, Pinon Press, Colorado Springs, Colorado.

Keck, Gregory C., Ph.D. and Kupecky, Regina M., LSW (2002) Parenting the Hurt Child: Helping Adoptive Families Heal and Grow, Pinon Press, Colorado Springs, Colorado.

Keller, Holly. (1991) Horace, William Morrow and Company, New York, New York.

Kubler-Ross, Elisabeth. (1969) On Death and Dying: What the Dying Have to Teach Doctors, Nurses, Clergy, and Their Own Families, Simon and Schuster, New York, New York.

Maslow, Abraham H. (1943) A Theory of Human Motivation, Psychological Review, 50, p. 370-396.

McAndrew, Laura. (1999) Little Flower: A Journey of Caring, Child Welfare League of America Press, Washington, D.C.

McCourt, Lisa. (1997) I Love You Stinky Face, Scholastic Cartwheel Books.

Moser, Adolph, Ed.D. (1991) Don't Feed the Monster on Tuesdays, Landmark House, Limited, Scottsdale, Arizona.

Nichols, Melissa, M.A., Lacher, Denise, M.A., May, Joanne, Ph.D. (2002) Parenting with Stories: Creating a Foundation of Attachment for Parenting Your Child, Family Attachment Center, Deephaven, Minnesota.

Orlans, Michael and Levy, Terry M. (2006) Healing Parents: Helping Wounded Children Learn to Trust and Love, Child Welfare League of America Press, Washington, D.C.

Pavao, Joyce Maguire. (2005) The Family of Adoption, Beacon Press, Boston, Massachusetts.

Penn, Audrey. (1993) The Kissing Hand, Scholastic, Inc. New York, New York.

Perry, Bruce D., M.D., Ph.D. and Szalavitz, Maia (2006) The Boy Who Was Raised as a Dog: What Traumatized Children Can Teach Us About Loss, Love, and Healing, Basic Books, New York, New York.

Reamer, Frederic G. (2003) Social Work Malpractice and Liability Strategies for Prevention, Columbia University Press, New York, New York.

Reamer, Frederic G. (October 2005) Social Work, Vol 50, No. 4, pp 325-334.

Reamer, Frederic G. (April 2005) Social Work, Vol 27, No. 2, pp 117-120.

Rosove, Lori. (2001) Rosie's Family: An Adoption Story, Asia Press, Ontario, Canada.

Saltz, Gail, M.D. (2005) Amazing You! Getting Smart About Your Private Parts, Penguin Group, New York, New York.

Seuss, Dr. (1990) Oh, The Places You'll Go!, Random House, New York, New York.

Siegel, Daniel J., M.D. (2013) Brainstorm: The Power and Purpose of the Teenage Brain, Penguin Group, New York.

Siegel, Daniel J., M.D. (1999) The Developing Mind: How Relationships and the Brain Interact to Shape Who We Are, The Guilford Press, New York, New York.

Siegel, Daniel J., M.D. (2007) The Mindful Brain: Reflection and Attunement in the Cultivation of Well-Being, W.W. Norton & Company, New York, New York.

Siegel, Daniel J. M.D. and Hartzell, Mary, M.ED. (2003) Parenting From The Inside Out: How a Deeper Self-Understanding Can Help You Raise Children Who Thrive, Jeremy P. Tarcher, Penguin, New York, New York.

Siegel, Daniel J., M.D. and Bryson, Tina Payne, Ph.D. (2011) The Whole-Brain Child: 12 Revolutionary Strategies to Nurture Your Child's Developing Mind, Delacorte Press, New York, New York.

Stein, Theodore J. (2004) The Role of Law in Social Work Practice and Administration, Columbia University Press, New York, New York.

Viorst, Judith. (1972) Alexander and the Terrible, Horrible, No Good, Very Bad Day, Atheneum Books for Young Readers, New York, New York.

Yalom, Irvin D. (2008) Staring at the Sun: Overcoming the Terror of Death, Jossey-Bass, San Francisco, California.

Appendices

Policies and Procedures

How much do you charge?

My rate is $120 per hour or we may agree on another rate. If you are using the mental health benefits of your insurance company, the insurance company will determine our agreed upon rate including any co-payment due at the time of the appointment. I also charge for consultation, supervision, treatment meetings, court testimony, and providing client records. The fee is due from the first session and for any sessions cancelled without notice. I may bill your insurance company directly and/or provide you with a bill/receipt.

How long does a therapy session last?

A session lasts about 45 minutes. I spend the rest of the hour preparing for our session and completing paperwork related to it. If we agree to longer or shorter sessions, my fee will be prorated. I may spend some time with you on the telephone at intake but I generally do not discuss issues over the telephone or by e-mail. I charge for appointments cancelled with less than 24 hours' notice and may reschedule appointments or terminate services for failure to follow this policy or failure to pay my fees.

How long will therapy take?

I really think in terms of time-limited work. Each period entails a specific piece of work. Each period has a beginning, middle, and end. If we accomplish our goals, our work is finished. If we have more work to do, we'll agree to another specific time frame. Sometimes this is determined by your insurance coverage. If it's a big issue, we'll break it down into manageable parts. Some problems take a few minutes, some a few sessions, some a few months, and sometimes a few years of ongoing work. Generally, appointments are weekly but we may agree to another schedule for work.

Therapy ends for a variety of reasons; treatment is complete, a planned break or pause, there is little or no progress, disagreement about treatment goals and interventions, client requires other services, client choice, therapist choice, violation of cancellation or payment policy, client files complaint or legal action against the therapist, client ends therapy without notice. When termination of services is planned I will ask for at least one closing session to process the decision, make recommendations and referrals, and suspend or end our work together. However, even after termination the therapist-client relationship continues including my responsibility to maintain your personal information, your confidentiality, privacy, and legal privilege.

What happens in therapy?

First, I want to get to know you and hear your concerns. Then, I'll explain how I work and we'll develop a plan. We'll decide together what you want to accomplish and how we will know if we are successful. Therapy includes talking, activities, and homework. During the first session I will review your personal information; explain confidentiality, mandated reporting, privacy, privilege; my documentation standards and recording keeping, share my practice model, ask assessment and safety questions, and hear your concerns. My interventions include assessment, risk management, diagnosis, treatment planning, crisis intervention, case management, and psycho-education. I employ a variety of techniques from motivational interviewing to role play as we work through our treatment plan toward evaluation and termination.

Therapy has both benefits and risks. The benefits may include self- acceptance, improved relationships, and reduction in unpleasant symptoms. The risks can include discomfort from facing difficult experiences and feelings and important decisions and changes in personal relationships. Personal growth and change can go fast or slow and things can get worse before better. You always have the option to seek alternatives or to end therapy at any time.

What makes you different from other therapists?

Just like every client, every therapist is unique. It's more about the relationship that you develop with your therapist. I'm open and friendly. I also like to use humor. I have unique training and experience. I have a very straight forward style. I work with individuals, couples, families, and groups. When I work with children and youth I include parents. I use psychodynamic and solution focused approaches, emotional focused and attachment therapy, and cognitive behavioral, play, and narrative techniques. I also provide consultation, supervision, and training for parents and clinicians. I can provide a list of other referrals and resources that may be helpful to you. I generally do not work with parents in conflict through legal proceedings.

What is your education and experience?

I graduated from Our Lady of the Lake University in San Antonio, Texas with a Master of Social Work degree. I became a Licensed Clinical Social Worker in California in 2004. I have been in private practice pre and post licensure since 2003. My experience and training includes the topics of adjustment, anxiety, depression, traumatic stress, parenting, child welfare, adoption, attachment, child development, couples communication, group processes, and supervision. I receive at least 18 hours of continuing education every two years. I belong to the National Association of Social Workers and pledge to uphold the Code of Ethics and to obey the laws of the State of California and the United States of America.

What are your personal beliefs, values, politics?

Feeling comfortable with a therapist is important and I want to foster that safe professional relationship with you. For some, that means knowing your therapist's marital, parenting, political, or religious status. The gender and ethnicity may be more apparent. However, I will not share this personal information with you. The reason is that I intend our professional relationship to be entirely about you and your needs. Thus, I will know more about you than you know about me. The therapist-client relationship is inherently unequal. I have more power and responsibility than you. A therapist cannot possibly have all the experiences of each and every client, and the individual meanings are not the same even if the experiences are. I commit to learn, understand, accept, and incorporate your identities, values, and beliefs and the meaning they have for your life. Further, I commit to keeping my personal beliefs and reactions from interfering with our work by self-examination, consultation, and supervision as necessary.

What is the best way to contact you?

Call or e-mail me to make an appointment, fill out the online forms and bring in the completed paperwork with you. If you plan to use your insurance coverage, check its panel of providers to make sure I am on the list. I make and receive telephone calls, e-mails, and faxes during regularly scheduled business hours only. I do not respond to texting. I am not available during non-business hours except by appointment. I am not available to respond to crisis and emergencies. For those, follow the directions on my telephone, website, e-mail, and fax messages to call 911 or go to the nearest hospital emergency room or call the San Diego Access and Crisis Line 1-888-724-7240. I will use the emergency number you provide to me to contact you in case of my emergency or designate a professional colleague to contact you for me.

What are your hours?

I'm available by appointment Monday and Friday 10:00 a.m. to 4:00 p.m. and Tuesday, Wednesday, Thursday 1:00 p.m. to 7:00 p.m.

Why is therapy necessary?

It isn't. But some problems, like trauma and mental illness, are so serious that therapy is the recommended treatment. Also, sometimes each of us gets kind of stuck. What's worked before or what we already know isn't enough. It's very helpful to go to an objective professional to give us fresh perspectives and help us apply some new knowledge and techniques to get unstuck. We seek attention for medical conditions. Mental health conditions deserve the same treatment. You may also choose no treatment or other resources and referrals I can provide to you upon request.

Can therapy help my relationship?

Yes, in two ways. First, it could help your relationship when the two of you come in together to talk about your communication, concerns and conflicts. If that is not possible, it could help your relationship if you come in to talk about your relationship history, your personality, your past relationships, and how you feel about yourself.

Do you do outcalls?

Under most circumstances, no. However, if parenting is the issue, it may be helpful for me to see the family in the home. If a client is in crisis or hospitalized, I may see him or her to continue treatment.

Why can't I just go see my doctor about my problem?

You may, however, doctors are for medical problems and psychotherapists are for psychological problems. A medical doctor usually doesn't have the time to talk through issues, while that's what we do in therapy.

Can you prescribe medications like my doctor?

No. If I feel that medications could help I will refer you to a doctor or a psychiatrist for a medication evaluation.

Who authorizes my participation in therapy?

If you are an adult and have the capacity to consent for your own treatment, you initiate therapy. If a court has appointed a conservator to act on your behalf, that person consents for your treatment. A parent, guardian, or other legal representative like a judge consents for therapy for a child unless the person is an emancipated youth or at least 12 years old and seeking treatment for substance use or sexual issues where informing parents might be dangerous. I will request that both parents with legal rights consent for a child's treatment, and will stop therapy if either parent withdraws consent. Each adult in a couple, family, or group consents to his/her own participation, and I keep personal information in separate client files. Your insurance company may have specific requirements for authorizing and paying for services, if you decide to use your benefits.

How do you handle my personal information?

I will not identify you by name in my waiting room, over the telephone, in unsolicited e-mail, facsimile, social media, or in public, not even with a partner or other family member. The therapist-client relationship is a professional one that makes me more responsible for protecting your personal information. It does not include any form of sexual activity or financial interactions like gifts in or out of the office. If we cross this professional boundary such as meeting in public or on line, participating in an activity in the community, or finding ourselves in any other dual relationship, I will raise the issue, check with you about this potential breach, and determine a way to maintain your confidentiality that is acceptable to both of us.

While your personal information is protected by laws governing confidentiality, privacy, and privilege, there are times when I am legally required to breach your confidentiality. These are my mandated reporting requirements for harm to self, others, or property, child abuse, elder abuse, disabled abuse, and animal abuse. Children do not have the right to privacy from their parents except when 12 years old or older seeking substance abuse or sexual treatment when informing parents may cause harm. When working with children, youth, couples, and families I have a no holding information policy, sometimes called a "no secrets policy", in that I will use my professional judgment in deciding whether, when, and how to share information that one client does not want another client to know. The exception is when the information is about STD/HIV/AIDS status.

I have password protected computer files, voicemail, and e-mail and keep client records, both paper and electronic, locked. I create a unique client file for you that includes identifying information, social history, assessments, symptoms, diagnoses, treatment plans, interventions, progress notes, and discharge reports. I keep these records for 10 years after we finish our work together or until a child client turns 28, then I destroy the files. You can have access to my information about you or request amendments to the information if you provide a written request. I may provide a written summary of your treatment and require that we talk about the information together. I charge for copying records.

If we decide it would be helpful for me to receive or share your information with another person or facility, I will ask you or your legal representative to sign an authorization for release or exchange of protected health information. I will not share your identifying information in supervision, consultation, trainings or research, and I will ask you to sign an authorization if your personal information or image might be disclosed. If I believe or learn that your personal information has been disclosed without your authorization, I will notify you in writing and take the necessary steps including filing a police report or destroying the information to limit the disclosure of your personal information.   I will respond to a subpoena to share your personal information by notifying you first, not disclosing any information, and responding only to court orders by claiming your legal privilege and seeking to limit disclosure of your information. This does not apply if you take legal action against me and I need to defend myself. I can legally share identifying information about you in order to collect fees for services. Your authorization to use your insurance benefits includes your consent for me to share your personal information including dates of services, diagnoses, and progress.

If I am unable to continue our professional relationship or to continue to maintain the privacy of your personal information in the future due to death or incapacitation, I have designated a professional colleague to notify you of this fact, to provide you with help in processing this information and your choices, to provide referrals for continuing your treatment as you choose, and to maintain the confidentiality of your personal information by managing the storage and destruction of my client files, to maintain my practice until I return and to close my business in the event of my death or incapacitation.

What if I don't like what happens in therapy?

Please let me know right away if something is not working for you. You are the customer of my services. Under most circumstances, like life, misunderstandings and differences of perception and opinion are normal. In fact, working through conflicts is part of therapy and can be helpful in and out of the office. I will often ask for feedback. Please be candid with me. You may raise your concerns in person or write a more formal complaint. I will often seek consultation without disclosing your personal information. We will work on a satisfactory solution together. If necessary, I will take your complaint to a panel of my professional colleagues and provide you their input. If this is not satisfactory, you may make a more formal complaint through your insurance provider whose policies I have promised to follow, the National Association of Social Workers, www.socialworkers.org, whose Code of Ethics I am sworn to uphold, or the California Board of Behavioral Sciences www.bbs.ca.gov, whose business and professional code I am required to follow.

How do you handle sensitive information like STD/HIV or immigration status?

While this information may be relevant to our work together including insurance authorization or treatment planning, please do not include it in any paperwork you provide to me. I will not document this information and will destroy any documentation I receive containing this information. I will ask you to sign an authorization for release or exchange of protected health information if you wish me to discuss this information with another person or facility or to specifically prohibit me from sharing this information. However, we will discuss this information in therapy if it is relevant to our work.

MICHAEL A. JONES
LICENSED CLINICAL SOCIAL WORKER

Michael A. Jones, LCSW 3511 Camino Del Rio South Suite 500
San Diego, California 92108 619-297-0010
LCSW22452
www.michaelajoneslcsw.com
askmike@michaelajoneslcsw.com

CLIENT INFORMATION

Your Name: _____

First Appointment Date:_____

Client Name (if different) :_____

Date of Birth:_____

For Minor Clients:

What is your relationship to the minor? (check all that apply)

☐ *Parent* ☐ *Legal Guardian* ☐ *Foster Parent* ☐ *Self* ☐ *Other*

Do you hold the legal privilege for this minor? ☐ *No* ☐ *Yes*
If no, who holds the legal privilege for this minor?

☐ *Parent* ☐ *Legal Guardian* ☐ *Court* ☐ *Minor* ☐ *Other*

Address: _____

City: _____ ZIP:_____

Home # ( ) _____-_____ Work # ( ) ____-_____

Emergency Contact:_____
Relationship: _____Telephone# (   )_____-_____

School/Employer:_____ Grade:_____
Contact:_____ Telephone:_____

Referral Source:_____ Telephone:_____

E-Mail_____

Payment Information:

Name of Insurance Company: _____

Telephone# _____

Member ID: _____

Group ID: _____Plan ID: _____

Authorization to see Michael A. Jones, LCSW_____

CoPay per visit:_____

☐ Provided Mental Health Services Information
☐ Provided Grievance and Appeal Procedures

Please list the names of the people (and pets) who live in your home:

	Name	Age	Relationship
1.			
2.			
3.			
4.			
5.			

Briefly, why are you seeking my services at this time ?

_____

_____

Medical History

Check all those that apply	Client	Relatives	DESCRIBE
Injuries to head			
Thyroid problems			
Diabetes or blood sugar issues			
Sexually transmitted disease			
Fainting/ loss of consciousness			
Allergies			
Physical impairment or handicap			
Menses – difficulties or irregular			Age of onset
Aches/pains (head, stomach, etc.)			
Medical Hospitalization			
Other Diseases			

Mental Health History

	Client	Relative	DESCRIBE
Depression			
Mania			
Risk Taking			
Behaviors			
Mental Health			
Hospitalization			
Therapy or Other			
Treatment			

Medications/Dosages:_____

Supplements/Vitamins:_____

Most recent Medical Exam: _____**Recommendations:**_____

Physician's Name: _____**Telephone #:**_____

Previous or Current Mental Health or Other Treatment Providers with Whom to Consult or Collaborate:

Dates Attended	Name of Provider Address/Telephone	Topics of Treatment

Life Stages History – Family History

In each section, please list the members of the household during that period in your life, and any events or experiences that you feel were significant, or impacted you positively or negatively, including any traumatic events. Please do not feel pressured to write down things that you do not wish to write about.

Client's mother's pregnancy history *(If you know anything about the mother's life experiences during her pregnancy, positive or negative, including her health and relationship with the father, please include it here.)*

Early Developmental Details (*ages 0-5 – ex: learning to talk, walk, use the bathroom, etc.*)

_____

_____

Childhood *(ages 6-12)*

_____

_____

Adolescence *(age 12 to 17)*

_____

_____

Young Adulthood *(ages 18 - 22)*

_____

_____

Adulthood *(ages 23 to present)*

_____

_____

Educational History

Schools Attended

_____

_____

Academic Performance (include special needs)

_____

_____

Friendships/ Peer Relationships in School

_____

_____

Spiritual/Cultural History

_____

_____

Legal History

(Ex: Arrests, Restraining Orders, Charges, Convictions, Sentences, Jail/Prison, Court Cases, Divorce, Child Custody)

_____

Current Symptoms – Please check, rate, describe:
0 (no symptoms) to 10 (severe)

PHYSICAL SYMPTOMS		Rating	Description
Sleeping Patterns			
Appetite			
Weight Change			
Elimination Concerns			
Fatigue			
Crying			
Sexual Energy Changes			
Aches and Pains			
Aggression			
Stealing			
Arguing/Rages			
Manipulation			

EMOTIONAL SYMPTOMS		Rating	Description
Hopelessness			
Decrease in Enjoyment/Interests			
Sadness			
Anger			
Fear			
Loneliness			
Preoccupation with Death			
Thoughts of Suicide			

COGNITIVE SYMPTOMS		Rating	Description
Traumatic memories			
Intrusive thoughts			
Flashbacks			
Dwelling or Daydreaming			
Self-blaming thoughts			
Worries interfere with life			
Ability to make decisions			
Ability to concentrate			

SOCIAL SYMPTOMS		Rating	Description
Isolation			
Easily irritated			
Decrease in friendships			
Conflict with family members			
Employment issues			
Financial Issues			
Legal Issues			

RISK ASSESSMENT	Yes	No	Explain
Do you intend to hurt yourself?			
Do you have a plan?			
Do you have means?			
Have you attempted self-harm?			
Do you intend to harm anyone?			
Have you identified that person?			
Do you have a plan?			
Do you have a means?			
Attempted to harm others?			
Alcohol/legal/illegal drug use?			
Age of first use?			
Date of last use?			
Frequency of use?			
Amount of last use?			
Duration of use?			
Difficulty stopping ?			

Concern about use?			
Consequences if use?			
Sought treatment?			
Relationship violence?			
Child abuse?			
Elder abuse?			
Disabled abuse?			
Animal abuse?			

Michael A. Jones, LCSW

INFORMED CONSENT
and CONFIDENTIALITY AGREEMENT

Introduction

This agreement is intended to provide _____ (*Client*) with important information regarding the practice policies and procedures of Michael A. Jones, LCSW (*Therapist*) and to clarify the terms of the professional therapeutic relationship between Client and Therapist. The Health Insurance Portability and Accountability Act of 1996 (*HIPPA*) requires that Client is provided with a Notice of Privacy Protection which is attached to this agreement. Any questions or concerns regarding the contents of this Agreement should be discussed with Therapist prior to signing it.

Therapist Education, Training, Experience, Theoretical Orientation, and Treatment Approaches

Therapist earned a master's degree (*MSW*) and has been licensed by the Board of Behavioral Sciences in California as a clinical social worker (*LCSW*) since December 15, 2004. Therapist participates in a minimum of 18 hours of continuing education every two years. Therapist has experience working with children, adolescents, adults, couples, families, groups and supervisees. Therapist employs treatment modalities based in attachment, developmental, psychodynamic, and cognitive-behavioral theories. In approaches targeting the parent-child relationship therapist may demonstrate, teach, and encourage the use of appropriate safe touch in care, nurturing, and play with children and adolescents. Therapy approaches with children, adolescents, couples and families most often require the participation of all parties in treatment. Therapist employs a time-limited approach based on diagnosis, prognosis, and mutually agreed upon modalities, established treatment goals, and behaviorally measurable progress. Therapist also employs a crisis management model including immediate assessment, referral, and possible ethical, legal, and medical coordination when immediate risk supersedes current treatment.

130

Benefits and Risks of Therapy

Psychotherapy is a process in which Client and Therapist explore and discuss a myriad of issues, events, experiences and memories for the purpose of creating positive change so Client can experience his/her life more fully. Psychotherapy is a joint effort between Client and Therapist. Progress and success may vary depending upon several factors, including but not limited to the types of issues or problems being explored and addressed, Client's personal history, Client's resources and support systems, and Client's level of motivation.

Participating in therapy may result in a number of benefits to Client, including, but not limited to, a reduction in stress, anxiety, and depression, a decrease in negative thoughts and self-sabotaging behaviors, improved interpersonal relationships, increased comfort in social, work and family settings, increased capacity for intimacy, and increased self-confidence. Such benefits may also require substantial effort on the part of Client, including an active participation in the therapeutic process, honesty, and a willingness to change thoughts, feelings, and behaviors. There is no guarantee that therapy will yield any or all of the benefits listed above.

Participating in therapy may also involve some discomfort, including remembering and discussing unpleasant events, feelings and experiences. The process may evoke strong feelings of sadness, guilt, anger, frustration, fear, loneliness, helplessness, and hopelessness. There may be times in which Therapist will challenge Client's perceptions and assumptions, and offer different perspectives. The issues presented by Client may result in unintended outcomes, including changes in personal relationships. Client should be aware that any decision on the status of his/her personal relationships is the responsibility of Client.

During the therapeutic process, many clients find that they feel worse before they feel better. This is generally a normal course of events. Personal growth and change may be easy and swift at times, but may also be slow and frustrating. Client should address

Michael A. Jones, LCSW

any concerns he/she has regarding his/her progress in therapy with Therapist.

Professional Consultation

Professional consultation is an important component of a healthy psychotherapy practice. As such, Therapist regularly participates in clinical, ethical, and legal consultation with appropriate professionals. During such consultations, Therapist will not reveal any personally identifying information regarding Client.

Records and Record Keeping

Therapist may take notes during session, and will also produce other notes and records regarding Client's treatment. These notes constitute Therapist's clinical and business records, which by law, Therapist is required to maintain. Such records are the sole property of Therapist. Therapist will not alter normal record keeping process at the request of any Client. Should Client request a copy of Therapist's records; such a request must be made in writing. Therapist reserves the right, under California law, to provide Client with a treatment summary in lieu of actual records. Therapist also reserves the right to refuse to produce a copy of the record under certain circumstances, but may, as requested, provide a copy of the record to another treating health care provider. Therapist will maintain Client's records for ten years following termination of therapy. However, after ten years, Client's records will be destroyed in a manner that preserves Client's confidentiality.

Confidentiality

The information disclosed by Client is generally confidential and will not be released to any third party without written authorization from Client, except when required or permitted by law. Exceptions to confidentiality include, but are not limited to, the *suspected abuse* of children (including by relationship violence), dependent adults, the elderly, and animals. Exceptions to confidentiality also include serious risk of *self injury* including suicide, the use of dangerous substances, and untreated medical conditions that could cause imminent death. Therapist also has a legal duty to warn the identified victim and report to police *intended harm* to persons and property. Therapist will work with Client to facilitate joint report when possible and to maintain the therapeutic relationship while providing only the information necessary to meet legal and ethical mandated reporting requirements.

When parents and children, couples, or families participate in therapy, the parent-child, couple, or family is the treatment unit. Therapist will maintain the confidentiality of each individual but cannot guarantee that all parties in the treatment unit will maintain confidentiality for the others. Therapist may meet with a smaller part of the treatment unit but uses his best clinical judgment to determine whether, when, and how to make disclosures of information learned in the separate session to the rest of the treatment unit, usually encouraging and facilitating the smaller unit to communicate the information to the rest of the treatment unit. If you feel it necessary to talk about matters you do not want to share with the rest of the treatment team, you may consider individual therapy. The addition of other parties to the treatment process will require each individual Client or Client representative to sign an Authorization for the Release of Protected Health Information or a renegotiation of the psychotherapy contract.

Client Litigation

Therapist will not voluntarily participate in any litigation, or custody dispute in which Client and another individual, or entity, are parties. Therapist has a policy of not communicating with Client's attorney and will generally not write or sign letters, reports, declarations, or affidavits to be used in Client's legal matters. Therapist will generally not provide records or testimony unless compelled to do so. Should Therapist be subpoenaed, or ordered by a court of law, to appear as a witness in an action involving Client, Client agrees to reimburse Therapist for any time spent for preparation, travel, or other time in which Therapist is available for such an appearance at Therapist's usual and customary hourly rate of **$120.00**.

Psychotherapist-Client Privilege

The information disclosed by Client, as well as any records created, is subject to the psychotherapist-client privilege. The psychotherapist-client privilege results from the special relationship between Therapist and Client in the eyes of the law. It is akin to the attorney-client privilege or the doctor-patient privilege. If Therapist receives a subpoena for records, deposition testimony, or testimony in a court of law, Therapist will assert the psychotherapist-client privilege on Client's behalf until instructed, in writing, to do otherwise by Client, Client's representative, or the Court. Client should be aware that he/she might be waiving the psychotherapist-client privilege if he/she makes his/her mental or emotional state an issue in a legal proceeding including those against the Therapist. Client should address concerns he/she might have regarding the psychotherapist-client privilege with an attorney.

Fee and Fee Arrangements

The usual and customary fee for service is **$120.00** per 45-minute session. Sessions longer than 45-minutes are charged for the additional time pro rata. Therapist reserves the right to periodically adjust this fee. Client will be notified of any fee adjustment in advance. In addition, this fee may be adjusted by contract with insurance companies, managed care organizations, or other third-party payors, or by agreement with Therapist. Clients are expected to pay for services at the time services are rendered unless other arrangements are made in advance. Therapist accepts cash and personal checks. Client will be charged **$25.00** if a check is returned from the bank due to insufficient funds. Thereafter, Client will be required to pay by cash only.

From time-to time, Therapist may engage in telephone contact with Client for purposes other than scheduling sessions. Client is responsible for payment of the agreed upon fee at a pro rata basis for any telephone calls longer than ten minutes.

Insurance

Client is responsible for full payment of all fees. If Client intends to use benefits of his/her health insurance policy, this must be agreed upon in advance by Client and Therapist. If Therapist is a contracted provider for the Client's insurance plan, Therapist will submit claims and required paperwork to be reimbursed by the insurance company. Client is responsible for verifying and understanding the limits of his/her coverage, as well as his/her co-payments and deductibles. Client is responsible to request initial authorization from his/her insurance plan. Client is responsible for payment of co-pays and deductibles at the time of the session. Use of the Client's insurance requires the signed Authorization for Release of Protected Health Information and Notice of Privacy Practices.

If Therapist is *NOT* a contracted provider for the Client's insurance plan, Client will be responsible for full payment at the time of the session. Client will be provided with a statement which Client can submit to his/her insurance company to seek reimbursement for fees already paid. Client agrees to inform Therapist in advance of any changes related to insurance coverage. Therapist is a contracted provider with several companies and has agreed to specified fees.

Cancellation Policy

Client is responsible for payment of the full fee for any session(s) not cancelled within 24 hours. Cancellation notice should be left on Therapist's voice mail at **(619) 297-0010.** If Client does not call to cancel a session and does not arrive at the scheduled time, Therapist will wait for *15 minutes*. At that time, if Client has not arrived or phoned to report a delay, the session will be considered non-attended and the fee will apply. In the event of a non-canceled and non-attended session, Client agrees to contact Therapist within seven days to schedule the next session. *Please note: the same day and session time may not be available.* If Client does not contact Therapist within seven days of a non-canceled and non-attended session, Therapist will assume that Client does not wish to continue therapy at that time. Client may contact Therapist to resume therapy if and when desired. When insurance prohibits late fees, Therapist will terminate service and provide referrals after two no show sessions.

Therapist Availability

Therapist's office is equipped with a confidential voice mail system that allows Client to leave a message at any time. Therapist will make every effort to return calls within 24 hour (or by the next business day), but cannot guarantee the calls will be returned immediately. Therapist is unable to provide 24-hour crisis service. *In the event that Client is feeling unsafe or requires immediate medical or psychiatric assistance, he/she should call 911, the Access and Crisis Line at (800) 479-3339, or go to the nearest emergency room*. Therapist's outgoing message will provide these same instructions. Therapist is routinely in the office Monday through Friday. *Sessions are by scheduled appointment only.* Therapist will inform Client of changes to the routine schedule.

Termination of Therapy

Client and Therapist may agree to end therapy when treatment goals are met. Therapist reserves the right to terminate therapy at Therapist's discretion. Reasons for termination include nonattendance, untimely payment, failure to comply with treatment recommendations, conflicts of interest, failure to participate in therapy, Client needs are outside the Therapist's scope of competence or practice, or Client is not making adequate progress in therapy. Client has the right to terminate therapy at his/her discretion. Upon either party's decision to terminate therapy, Therapist will generally recommend that Client participate in at least one termination session. These sessions are intended to facilitate a positive termination experience and give both parties an opportunity to reflect on the work done and make appropriate recommendations. Therapist will also attempt to ensure a smooth transition to another therapist by offering referrals and making himself available for continuity of care. Therapist has made provisions for notifying clients, providing referrals, and maintaining client records in the event of Therapist death, disability, or business closure.

Acknowledgement

By signing below, Client acknowledges that he/she has reviewed and fully understands the terms and conditions of this Agreement. Client has discussed such terms and conditions with Therapist, and has had any questions with regard to its terms and conditions answered to Client's satisfaction. Client agrees to abide by the terms and conditions of this Agreement and consents to participate in psychotherapy with Therapist. Moreover, Client agrees to hold Therapist free and harmless from any claims, demands, or suits for damages from any injury or complications whatsoever, save negligence, that may result from such treatment.

_____
Client Name (please print)

_____
Signature of Client (or authorized representative)

Date:_____

I understand that I am financially responsible to Therapist for all charges, including unpaid charges by my insurance company or any other third-party payor.

_____
Name of Responsible Party (please print)

Signature of Responsible Party:_____

Date:_____

NOTICE OF PRIVACY PRACTICES

THIS NOTICE DESCRIBES HOW MEDICAL INFORMATION ABOUT YOU MAY BE USED AND DISCLOSED AND HOW YOU CAN GET ACCESS TO THIS INFORMATION.
PLEASE REVIEW THIS NOTICE CAREFULLY.

Your health record contains personal information about you and your health. This information, which may identify you and relates to your past, present or future physical or mental health or condition and related health care services, is referred to as Protected Health Information ("PHI"). This Notice of Privacy Practices describes how we may use and disclose your PHI in accordance with applicable law. It also describes your rights regarding how you may gain access to and control your PHI.

We are required by law to maintain the privacy of PHI and to provide you with notice of our legal duties and privacy practices with respect to PHI. We are required to abide by the terms of this Notice of Privacy Practices. We reserve the right to change the terms of our Notice of Privacy Practices at any time. Any new Notice of Privacy Practices will be effective for all PHI that we maintain at that time. We will provide you with a copy of the revised Notice of Privacy Practices by posting a copy on our website, sending a copy to you in the mail upon request, or providing one to you at your next appointment.

HOW WE MAY USE AND DISCLOSE HEALTH INFORMATION ABOUT YOU:

For Treatment. Your PHI may be used and disclosed by those who are involved in your care for the purpose of providing, coordinating, or managing your health care treatment and related services. This includes consultation with clinical supervisors or other treatment team members. We may disclose PHI to any other consultant only with your authorization.

For Payment. We may use or disclose PHI so that we can receive payment for the treatment services provided to you. This will only be done with your authorization. Examples of payment-related activities are: making a determination of eligibility or coverage for insurance benefits, processing claims with your insurance company, reviewing services provided to you to determine medical necessity, or undertaking utilization review activities. If it becomes necessary to use collection processes due to lack of payment for services, we will only disclose the minimum amount of PHI necessary for purposes of collection.

For Health Care Operations. We may use or disclose, as needed, your PHI in order to support our business activities including, but not limited to, quality assessment activities, employee review activities, reminding you of appointments, to provide information about treatment alternatives or other health related benefits and services, licensing, and conducting or arranging for other business activities. For example, we may share your PHI with third parties that perform various business activities (e.g., billing or typing services) provided we have a written contract with the business that requires it to safeguard the privacy of your PHI. For training or teaching purposes PHI will be disclosed only with your authorization.

Required by Law. Under the law, we must make disclosures of your PHI to you upon your request. In addition, we must make disclosures to the Secretary of the Department of Health and Human Services for the purpose of investigating or determining our compliance with the requirements of the Privacy Rule.

Following is a list of the categories of uses and disclosures permitted by HIPAA without an authorization.

Abuse and Neglect	**Judicial and Administrative**
Emergencies	**Law Enforcement**
National Security	**Public Safety (Duty to Warn)**

Without Authorization. Applicable law and ethical standards permit us to disclose information about you without your authorization only in a limited number of other situations. The types of uses and disclosures that may be made without your authorization are those that are

- Required by law, such as the mandatory reporting of child abuse or neglect or mandatory government agency audits or investigations (such as the social work licensing board or health department)
- Required by Court Order
- Necessary to prevent or lessen a serious and imminent threat to the health or safety of a person or the public. If information is disclosed to prevent or lessen a serious threat, it will be disclosed to a person or persons reasonably able to prevent or lessen the threat, including the target of the threat.

Verbal Permission. We may use or disclose your information to family members that are directly involved in your treatment with your verbal permission.

With Authorization. Uses and disclosures not specifically permitted by applicable law will be made only with your written authorization, which may be revoked.

YOUR RIGHTS REGARDING YOUR PHI

You have the following rights regarding your personal PHI maintained by our office. To exercise any of these rights, please submit your request in writing to our Privacy Officer: Michael A. Jones, LCSW 3511 Camino Del Rio South Suite 500, San Diego, California 92108, 619-297-0010.

- **Right of Access to Inspect and Copy.** You have the right, which may be restricted only in exceptional circumstances, to inspect and copy PHI that may be used to make decisions about your care. Your right to inspect and copy PHI will be restricted only in those situations where there is compelling evidence that access would cause serious harm to you. We may charge a reasonable, cost-based fee for copies.
- **Right to Amend.** If you feel that the PHI we have about you is incorrect or incomplete, you may ask us to amend the information, although we are not required to agree to the amendment.
- **Right to an Accounting of Disclosures.** You have the right to request an accounting of certain of the disclosures that we make of your PHI. We may charge you a reasonable fee if you request more than one accounting in any 12-month period.
- **Right to Request Restrictions.** . You have the right to request a restriction or limitation on the use or disclosure of your PHI for treatment, payment, or health care operations. We are not required to agree to your request unless the request is to restrict disclosure of PHI to a health plan for purposes of carrying out payment or health care operations, and the PHI pertains to a health care item or service that you paid for out of pocket. In that case, we are required to honor your request for a restriction.
- **Right to Request Confidential Communication.** You have the right to request that we communicate with you

about medical matters in a certain way or at a certain location.

- **Breach Notification.** If there is a breach of unsecured protected health information concerning you, we may be required to notify you of this breach, including what happened and what you can do to protect yourself
- **Right to a Copy of this Notice.** You have the right to a copy of this notice.

COMPLAINTS

If you believe we have violated your privacy rights, you have the right to file a complaint in writing with our Privacy Officer, or with the Secretary of Health and Human Services at 200 Independence Avenue, S.W., Washington, D.C. 20201, or by calling (202) 619-0257.

We will not retaliate against you for filing a complaint.

The effective date of this Notice is _____

Notice of Privacy Practices
Receipt and Acknowledgment of Notice

**Client
Name:**_____

Date of Birth:

_____

I hereby acknowledge that I have received and have been given an opportunity to read a copy of the Privacy Practices of Michael A. Jones, LCSW.

I understand that if I have any questions regarding the Notice or my privacy rights, I can contact the Privacy Officer, Michael A. Jones, LCSW.

_____

Signature of Client

_____

Signature of Parent, Guardian or Personal Representative*

_____

Date

* If you are signing as a personal representative of an individual, please describe your legal authority to act for this individual (power of attorney, healthcare surrogate, etc.).

❑   Patient/Client Refuses to Acknowledge Receipt:

_____

Signature of Staff Member   Date

MICHAEL A. JONES
LICENSED CLINICAL SOCIAL WORKER

Camino Del Rio South Suite 500
San Diego, California 92108
PH: (619) 297-0010   Fax: (619) 624-0178
askmike@michaelajoneslcsw.com

AUTHORIZATION TO RELEASE OR EXCHANGE CONFIDENTIAL INFORMATION

A. Person or facility:
    Name_____

Address_____

Telephone
Number_____

B. Client Information:

C. Name_____

Address_____

Telephone
Number_____

Birthdate_____

Parent/Guardian_____

Address_____

Telephone
Number_____

D. I hereby authorize the source named above to send, as promptly as possible, only the records marked below. Page numbers may be indicated. Dates indicate when information is sent.

  o Inpatient or outpatient treatment records for physical and/or psychological, psychiatric, emotional illness, or substance abuse:_____

- o Psychological evaluations or testing, behavioral observations or checklists completed by any staff member or by the client:_____
- o Psychiatric evaluations, reports, or treatment notes and summaries:_____
- o Treatment Plans, recovery plans, aftercare, safety plans:_____
- o Admission and discharge summaries:_____
- o Social histories, assessments with diagnoses, prognoses, recommendations, and all other similar documents:_____
- o Information about how the client's condition affects or has affected his or her ability to complete tasks, activities of daily living, or ability to work:_____
- o Workshop reports and other vocational evaluations and reports:_____
- o Billing records:_____
- o Academic or educational records:_____
- o Reports of teachers' observations:_____
- o Achievement and other test results:_____
- o A letter containing dates of treatment and summary of progress:_____
- o HIV-related and alcohol and drug information contained in these records will be released under this consent unless indicated here:_____
- o Other:_____

E. I authorize the source named above to speak by telephone with the professional identified in part N about the reasons for the client's referral, any relevant history or diagnoses, and other similar information that can assist with the client receiving treatment or being evaluated or referred elsewhere.

F. I understand that no services will be denied the client solely because I refuse to consent to this release of information, and that I am not in any way obligated to release these records. I do release them because I believe that they are necessary to assist in the development of the best possible treatment plan for the client. The information disclosed may be used in connections with the client's treatment.

G. This authorization to release confidential information is being made in compliance with the terms of the Privacy Act of 1974, the Freedom of Information Act of 1974, and pursuant to Federal Rules of Evidence. This form is to serve as both a general authorization, and a special authorization to release information under the Drug Abuse Office and Treatment Act of 1972, the Comprehensive Alcohol Abuse and Alcoholism Prevention, Treatment, and Rehabilitation Act Amends of 1974, the Veterans Omnibus Health Care Act of 1976, the Veterans Benefit and Services Act of 1988. It is also in compliance with Public Law 93-282, which prohibits further disclosure without the express written consent of the person to whom it pertains, or as otherwise permitted by such regulations. I understand that if the person or organization that receives this information is not a health care provider or health insurer the information may no longer by protected by federal privacy regulations. It is in compliance with the Health Insurance Portability and Accountability Act of 1996.

H. In consideration of this consent, I hereby release the source of the records from any and all liability arising therefrom.

I. This authorization is valid during the pendency of any claim or demand made by or in behalf of the client, and arising out of an accident, injury, or occurrence to the client. I understand that I may void this authorization, except for action already taken, at any time by means of a written letter revoking the authorization and transfer of information, but that this revocation is not retroactive. If I do not void this authorization, it will automatically expire within one year of the date I signed it.

J. I agree that a photocopy of this form is acceptable, but it must be individually signed by me, the client or my representative, and a witness if necessary.

K. I have been informed of the risk to privacy and limitations to confidentiality of the use of electronic means of information transfer, and I accept these risks.

L. I affirm that everything in this form that was not clear to me has been explained. I also understand that I have the right to receive a copy of this form upon my request.

M. Signatures:

Client   Printed Name   Date

Client Representative Printed Name Relationship Date

Witness   Printed Name Relationship Date

I, a mental health professional, have discussed the issues above with the patient/and or his/her parent or guardian. My observations of behavior and responses give me no reason to believe that this person is not fully competent to give informed and willing authorization.

Professional   Printed Name   Date

ASSESSMENT

DATE:
START/END TIME:
FREQUENCY:

MODALITY:

MSE:

Chief Complaint:

Initial Assessment:

DIAGNOSIS

TREATMENT PLAN

Target Issue:

Method:

Outcome Goal:

Measure:

Prognosis:

Consultations:

Medical Information:

Medications:

Coordination of Care:

Michael A. Jones, LCSW

PROGRESS NOTE

Target Symptoms and Changes:

Treatment Provided:

Progress and Prognosis:

Client's Affect, Behavior, Response or Reaction to Clinical Interventions.

Treatment Planned:

Michael A. Jones, LCSW

LEGAL/ETHICAL

Observation

MSE
History
Family History
Therapy History
Behavior
Referrals

Risk Reduction Actions
Circumstances:
Names
Dates
Times

Reasons for Legal/Ethical Action

Michael A. Jones, LCSW

DISCHARGE SUMMARY

REASON FOR TERMINATION
Treatment Plan completed
Little or no progress
Client refused to cooperate with treatment
Client ended therapy without notice
Client violated cancellation/payment policy
This is a planned pause in treatment
Client requires services not available here, referral made to:

TERMINATION DECISION
Therapist initiated
Client initiated
Mutual decision
Insurance ended
Other

TREATMENT SESSIONS
Referral Date
First Session
Last Session
Number of Sessions
Number of Sessions Cancelled
Number of No Shows

SERVICES PROVIDED
Individual
Couple
Family
Parent-Child,
Group
Consultation
Supervision
Other

ENDING DIAGNOSES

TREATMENT PLAN

GOAL

OUTCOME
No Change
Slight Change
Moderate Change
Very Good
Exceeded Expectations
Unable to Determine

Michael A. Jones, LCSW

MICHAEL A. JONES
LICENSED CLINICAL SOCIAL WORKER

Camino Del Rio South Suite 500
San Diego, California 92108
PH: (619) 297-0010 / Fax: (619) 624-0178
askmike@michaelajoneslcsw.com

Thank you for the opportunity to be helpful to you.

If you were satisfied with my services I would be happy to resume our work or to see anyone you choose to refer to me.

If I do not hear from you within 30 days, I will be closing your case and ending our work together. If an emergency arises in the interim, I am available to assist you. Resuming treatment will require a new intake with updated information. If you would like another provider, I am referring you to the San Diego Access and Crisis Line at 1-888-724-7240, sandiego.networkofcare.org, or your health insurance provider.

I continue to be responsible for protecting your confidentiality, privacy, and privilege within applicable laws. I will send copies of your records to those you authorize to receive them.

Sincerely,

Michael A. Jones, LCSW

MIKE'S FAMILY CHART

RIGHTS

Affection
Play

Food
Clothes
Home
Bed
Medical
School

EXPECTATIONS

Everybody stays safe
Use please, thank you,
excuse me, I'm sorry
Clean up after yourself
Ask before borrowing
Return it the way you got
 Do chores
 Attend family meetings
 Accept "No" for an answer

SCHEDULE

6:30 a.m. – Wake Up
6:45 a.m. – Make Bed
7:00 a.m. – Get Dressed
7:15 a.m. – Breakfast
7:45 a.m. – To School and Work
8:00 a.m. – School and Work
11:00 a.m. – Do Chores
12:00 p.m. – Lunch
1:00 p.m. – Rest Time
2:00 p.m. – School and Work
3:00 p.m. – Homework
4:00 p.m. – Book Time
5:00 p.m. – Play Time
6:00 p.m. – Dinner
7:00 p.m. – Bath
7:30 p.m. – Book
8:00 p.m. – Bed

PRIVILEGES

Dessert
Stay up late
Television
Computer
Games
Music
Stay Over
Movies
Fun Trips
Shopping

TEACHING

Natural
Redo
Make Amends
Say You're Sorry
Fix the Problem
Do Extra Chores

ABOUT THE AUTHOR

Michael A. Jones, LCSW is a therapist, trainer, and lecturer in San Diego. Michael was licensed by the California Board of Behavioral Sciences December 15, 2004. He has worked since 1999 with traumatized children and their families. Michael trains parents, case workers, students, and clinicians in the areas of attachment, adoption, parenting, solution focused treatment, and trauma informed care.

Michael works in private practice and as a faculty lecturer at San Diego State University School of Social Work. He also provides independent training and supervision toward LCSW licensure. Michael was an administrator for a foster family agency and two group homes for nearly three years. He was voted undergraduate field instructor of the year at SDSU in 2006.

Michael earned his master's degree in social work from Our Lady of the Lake University in San Antonio, Texas. Before becoming a social worker, Michael was a television reporter, anchor, producer, and editor for 15 years in Illinois, Tennessee, Oklahoma, and Texas.

www.ingramcontent.com/pod-product-compliance
Lightning Source LLC
Chambersburg PA
CBHW070344270326
41926CB00017B/3986